T0277121

Cambridge Elements ☰

Elements in the Philosophy of Ludwig Wittgenstein
edited by
David G. Stern
University of Iowa

WITTGENSTEIN
AND ETHICS

Anne-Marie Søndergaard Christensen
University of Southern Denmark

CAMBRIDGE
UNIVERSITY PRESS

Shaftesbury Road, Cambridge CB2 8EA, United Kingdom

One Liberty Plaza, 20th Floor, New York, NY 10006, USA

477 Williamstown Road, Port Melbourne, VIC 3207, Australia

314–321, 3rd Floor, Plot 3, Splendor Forum, Jasola District Centre,
New Delhi – 110025, India

103 Penang Road, #05–06/07, Visioncrest Commercial, Singapore 238467

Cambridge University Press is part of Cambridge University Press & Assessment,
a department of the University of Cambridge.

We share the University's mission to contribute to society through the pursuit of
education, learning and research at the highest international levels of excellence.

www.cambridge.org
Information on this title: www.cambridge.org/9781009467780

DOI: 10.1017/9781009439817

First published 2024

A catalogue record for this publication is available from the British Library.

ISBN 978-1-009-46778-0 Hardback
ISBN 978-1-009-43977-0 Paperback
ISSN 2632-7112 (online)
ISSN 2632-7104 (print)

Wittgenstein and Ethics

Elements in the Philosophy of Ludwig Wittgenstein

DOI: 10.1017/9781009439817
First published online: February 2024

Anne-Marie Søndergaard Christensen
University of Southern Denmark

Author for correspondence: Anne-Marie Søndergaard Christensen,
amsc@sdu.dk

Abstract: In Ludwig Wittgenstein's writings, ethics takes a central place. This Element investigates his engagement with ethics in both early and later thinking. Starting from the remarks on ethics in the *Tractatus Logico-Philosophicus* and the framing of these remarks, this Element presents two influential approaches to Tractarian ethics before it develops a coherent reading of ethics in the early thinking, focusing on ethical silence and the relationship notions of world and the philosophical 'I'. The reading of 'A Lecture on Ethics' focuses on the critique of ethical theory and the personal dimension of ethics, two themes also running through Wittgenstein's later thinking. It considers Wittgenstein's later ethical investigations, of ethical examples, ethically relevant language uses of language, and the connections between reflections on ethics and living. It also considers the role of the other in Wittgenstein's later thinking.

Keywords: Ludwig Wittgenstein, ethics, Tractatus Logico-Philosophicus, moral philosophy, ethical/moral language

ISBNs: 9781009467780 (HB), 9781009439770 (PB), 9781009439817 (OC)
ISSNs: 2632-7112 (online), 2632-7104 (print)

Contents

1 Wittgenstein's Remarks on Ethics

1.1 Wittgenstein on Ethics: Interpretative Challenges

Ludwig Wittgenstein was a morally serious person. His diaries attest his aspiration to be morally decent and his regrets and embarrassment over what he sees as his own moral failings as well as his reflections on the task of meeting his own ethical ideals. As he writes in an entry in 1937, 'life is far more serious than it looks like at the surface. Life is frightfully serious' (PPO: 175).[1] For Wittgenstein, the hardest challenge was to escape the temptation of moral self-delusion and come to see his own moral standing clearly. In the diaries, he exclaims: 'How difficult it is to know oneself, to honestly admit what one is!' (PPO: 221). But even at such moments, in the middle of the pursuit of self-understanding, Wittgenstein also often doubts his own sincerity and commitment, reproaching himself: 'Self-recognition & humility is one. (These are cheap remarks.)' (PPO: 105).

We find testimonies of the same aspiration for moral earnestness and determination in many recollections of Wittgenstein. His student and friend Norman Malcolm writes that 'Wittgenstein had an intense desire for moral and spiritual purity. "Of course I want to be perfect!" he exclaimed. This was not arrogance – for he knew he was far from perfect' (Malcolm 1993: 21). And Wittgenstein's close friend Paul Engelmann also notes Wittgenstein's uncompromising approach to his own moral standing, describing him as having an attitude of 'an ethical totalitarianism in all questions, a single-minded and painful preservation of the purity of the uncompromising demands of ethics, in agonizing awareness of one's own permanent failure to measure up to them' (EN: 109). Wittgenstein's moral seriousness is also reflected in his philosophical work and his conception of the activity of philosophy, which he sees as guided by not just ideals of clarity of thinking but also ethical ideals of attention and integrity. 'Don't apologize for anything, don't obscure anything, look & tell how it really is – but you must see something that sheds a new light on the facts' (CV: 45 [39]).[2] Philosophy comes with an obligation to exercise rigorous and truthful attention to the phenomena in one's interest, but for the philosopher to live up to this ideal, they need continuously to reflect on their own expectations and preconceived ideas of what may deserve attention, be important or valuable and so on. 'Work on philosophy ... is really more work on oneself. On one's own conception. On how one sees things. (And what one expects of them.)' (CV: 24 [16]). In this way, Wittgenstein thought that his philosophical work should influence his own moral standing: 'The movement of my thoughts in my philosophizing should be

---

[1] For abbreviations of Wittgenstein's works, see References.

[2] I refer to the 1998 edition of for *Culture and Value*, but references to the 1980 edition are added in square brackets.

discernible also in the history of my mind, of its moral concepts & in the understanding of my situation' (PPO: 133).

The centrality of ethics in Wittgenstein's life and its intimate connection to his way of doing philosophy seem to be a promising starting point for an Element such as this. There is, however, one challenge that faces any attempt to write rather concisely about Wittgenstein's view of ethics, which has shaped the surrounding interpretative landscape and will also influence the layout of this Element – the challenge that Wittgenstein wrote only little on ethics. In his own writings, the remarks that explicitly address topics of ethics and moral philosophy consist mainly of a group of remarks towards the ending of *Tractatus Logico-Philosophicus*, a manuscript published under the title 'A Lecture on Ethics' from 1929, one remark in the Philosophical Investigations (§77), and a number of rather scattered remarks in Wittgenstein's *Nachlass* and diaries, most of which are published in *Public and Private Occasions* and *Culture and Value*. To this, we can add at least two other sources. These are first and foremost discussions of issues related to ethics, the word 'good' and value recorded by students in notes from that Wittgenstein's lectures; now edited and published in several volumes (see e.g. LC, AWL, MWL). The second additional source is remarks that Wittgenstein made in public or personal conversations, documented by students and friends (see e.g. Waismann 1965, 1979; Rhees 1965; Malcolm 1984, 1993; Bouwsma 1986). At first sight, this may seem to constitute the foundation on which an interpreter will have to build an understanding of Wittgenstein's view of ethics. We do, however, also have a third and much more abundant resource, namely Wittgenstein's writings on other subjects such as the activity of philosophy, meaning, logic and grammar, and inner and outer. As we will come to see, these writings play a central role in the attempt to understand Wittgenstein's view of ethics and its place in the context of his wider philosophical endeavours.

The scarcity of textual resources and the challenges connected to the developments in Wittgenstein's work generally have led to extensive and complicated interpretative discussions about how to understand Wittgenstein's view of ethics and related issues (for overviews, see e.g. Johnston 1989; Lovibond 1998; Christensen 2011a). In fact, scholarship in this field is still growing significantly and involves substantial disagreement about many central issues, even about whether it makes sense to talk about something like Wittgenstein's 'view' of ethics. Scholars also disagree about whether Wittgenstein's own remarks on ethics should take centre stage in the attempt to develop a Wittgensteinian view of ethics, or whether the more important project is to develop the ethical implications of Wittgenstein's (early or later) philosophical work, more or less independently of an understanding of his own, admittedly, rather elusive view of ethics. Some scholars taking this stance simply turn to the task of developing the ethical implications of parts of Wittgenstein's writings that do not directly address ethical issues such as aspect seeing or his remarks on certainty (for examples, see Kober 2008; Pleasants 2008). In this Element, I will attempt to work out the best interpretation of Wittgenstein's own view of ethics, but discussions of how to understand Wittgenstein's work in philosophy more generally will inevitably also seep into and influence this interpretation.

1.2 Why Bother with Wittgenstein's Remarks on Ethics?

As work on Wittgenstein's view of ethics faces considerable interpretive challenges, it is reasonable to ask why we should take the trouble to even consider this view. This Element and other interpretative efforts put into Wittgenstein's remarks on ethics are, in a certain sense, attempts to answer this question, and whether these answers are sufficient is above all something for readers to decide. Still, I find it possible to offer at least two general reasons for why it may be fruitful to put in the effort of engaging with Wittgenstein's approach to ethics. The first is that the extensive interpretative debate surrounding this approach has made substantial contributions to Wittgenstein scholarship. The second is that Wittgenstein's approach differs radically from most other available approaches in moral philosophy in a way that gives us cause to challenge and rethink dominant conceptions of ethics in fruitful ways.

Still, the challenges in engaging with Wittgenstein's view of ethics persist, and they have influenced the basic interpretative principles guiding my approach as well as the way this Element is composed. The first guiding principle is to focus primarily on Wittgenstein's own sparse remarks on ethics, through close readings of central passages and consideration of their place within his wider oeuvre. This approach best reflects the importance of the original writings and enables me to ask whether and how Wittgenstein's remarks constitute a comprehensive approach to moral life. My second guiding principle is to try to place my own reading of Wittgenstein's remarks in relation to existing interpretations of Wittgensteinian ethics, especially in relation to the early writings. I thus begin the investigation of ethics in the *Tractatus* by quoting the remarks on ethics and presenting the two dominant approaches, the metaphysical and the resolute readings, before I develop what I think is the most coherent and loyal interpretation of Wittgenstein's early view of ethics. In chapter 4, I present a close reading of Wittgenstein's most sustained engagement with ethics in 'A Lecture on Ethics', together with two ideas that remain constant throughout his engagement with ethics, a critical approach to moral theorising and an emphasis on the personal dimension of ethics. In chapter 5, I discuss remarks on ethics from Wittgenstein's later writings. I will argue that while some aspects of Wittgenstein's view of ethics stay the same throughout his thinking, the changes in his later work also result in changes in how he thought philosophy could engage with ethics, making him give up the Tractarian view that ethics is not an appropriate subject for philosophical inquiry (contrary to e.g. Richter 1996, 2019).

2 Remarks on Ethics in the *Tractatus*: Guides and Interpretations

2.1 Wittgenstein's Main Contention

At the outbreak of the First World War, Wittgenstein volunteered as a soldier in the Austrian army, and during this time, serving first behind the front and later at the very frontline, he did much of the writing of what eventually became his first main book, *Tractatus Logico-Philosophicus* (Monk 1991: 137–66). Wittgenstein developed the work on the role of logic in thinking and language that he had begun as a student at Cambridge, but during his wartime experience, his philosophical writings changed character and new themes began to appear (Klagge 2021). We can follow this development in Wittgenstein's notebooks, when in June of 1916, after a month with no entries, he suddenly writes: 'What do I know about God and the purpose of life?' (NB: 72). After this time, Wittgenstein's entries are almost as much concerned with questions related to meaning of life, self, God, and value as they are with logic, and it is writing from this period that was eventually transformed into the very last part of the *Tractatus* where we find the remarks on ethics.

   The aim of this section and the next is to present Wittgenstein's early approach to ethics, and entries in the *Notebooks* offer us a valuable insight into the development of this approach. Still, I will not discuss these for two reasons. Most importantly, the *Tractatus* is comprised of remarks chosen and organised by Wittgenstein for publication, and it thus constitutes the most authoritative presentation of his view of ethics at this time. Moreover, involving the *Notebooks* almost inevitable gives rise to a discussion of whether or how the *Notebooks* remarks, the result of Wittgenstein's immediate and unedited first struggles with ethical issues, relate to the published work, and these reflections will inevitably divert attention from my main aim of trying to unfold the view of ethics that Wittgenstein intended to offer to readers of the *Tractatus*. I therefore focus on remarks published in the *Tractatus* together with remarks made by Wittgenstein in discussions following the publication of this work as well as the manuscript 'A Lecture on Ethics', which in my view marks the end of and a partial departure from the early period of Wittgenstein's thinking on ethics.

   Even if Wittgenstein wrote very little on ethics in the *Tractatus*, it is also evident that he considered ethics important and, in some way, central to his philosophical work. After finishing the manuscript for his book, Wittgenstein searched – for a period in vain – for the right place to publish it, and in a letter to a potential publisher, Ludwig von Ficker, he highlights the central importance of ethics for his work:

> The book's point is an ethical one. I once meant to include in the preface a sentence which is not in fact there now but which I will write out for you here . . .. My work consists of two parts: the one presented here plus all that I have *not* written. And it is precisely this second part that is the important one. My book draws limits to the ethical [*das Ethische*] from the inside as it were, and I am convinced that this is the ONLY *rigorous* way of drawing those limits. In short, I believe that where *many* others today are just *gassing*, I have managed in my book to put everything firmly into place by being silent about it. (EN: 143; translation amended)

The letter is quite surprising. Wittgenstein writes that, despite the fact that he has written only a few pages relating to matters of value and ethics at the very end of *Tractatus*, the engagement with these issues is a driving motivation behind the work. Moreover, he insists that the best way to honour this motivation is by *not* writing about ethics, and in contrast to others writing about ethics, that this is the only way to draw limits to what is ethical and to do so in the right way, by being silent.

To take Wittgenstein's letter seriously is to develop an interpretation of the *Tractatus* that begins from the acknowledgement that he approaches ethics as something that is quite distinct from what we normally talk *about* when we take ourselves to be talking about moral matters in an ordinary sense of 'talking about something'. It is also to acknowledge that in developing such an interpretation, we are in a sense working against Wittgenstein's concern with staying silent, because we will only be able to engage with his remarks on ethics by talking – or writing – about them. The present interpretative endeavour thus comes with an inbuilt conflict or even inconsistency at its very core because it, like other attempts to understand ethics in the *Tractatus*, necessarily goes beyond the silence recommended by Wittgenstein. In fact, a similar dilemma arises in relation to the *Tractatus* itself because, as Chon Tejedor notes, 'if ethics cannot be put into words . . ., how can a book – something that is, on the face of it, made up of words – have an ethical dimension?' (2010: 86). I will return to this tension between investigation and silence continuously in my engagement with the *Tractatus*.

The letter to Ludwig von Ficker is also interesting because Wittgenstein goes on to offer a form of 'guide' for reading his work, writing: 'Only perhaps you won't see that it is said in the book. For now, I would recommend you to read the *preface* and the *conclusion*, because they contain the most direct expression of the point of the book' (EN: 144). Wittgenstein thus seems to assume that it is possible – at least to some extent – to approach his view of ethics without having to engage in any substantial way with the main part of the *Tractatus*. This advice comes with an interpretative challenge, however. It is quite easy to identify the preface of the *Tractatus*, to which we will turn in a moment, as this is clearly marked and quite distinct in character from the rest of the work. However, the rest of the *Tractatus* consists of main remarks marked with numbers from 1 to 7, each followed by commenting remarks marked with decimal numbers. The problem is that none of the numbered remarks is singled out in any way; there is no special section titled 'Conclusion', and there is no other indication of what Wittgenstein could be alluding to here. One convention within Wittgenstein scholarship is to understand 'conclusion' as referring to the remarks beginning from 6.4, where Wittgenstein turns to discussions of value, ethics, the problem of life, death, God, what is mystical, and the right method of philosophy. In my view, an equally viable interpretation is to understand Wittgenstein's mention of conclusion as covering all of the remarks from 6 and onwards, both because the 6s constitute a whole section and because 7 is solitary, not followed by any remarks. This interpretation is supported by the fact that Wittgenstein, after the introduction of the general form of a proposition in 6, has a general undertaking. He works through the implications of his logical analysis for *philosophical* treatments of logic (6.1s), mathematics (6.2s), law (or necessity) and contingency (6.3s), and value (6.4s). In what follows, I therefore take all these remarks to constitute Wittgenstein's 'conclusion', and I place my main focus here, even if I also draw in other sections of the *Tractatus*.

There are other places where Wittgenstein mentions his general aim in writing the *Tractatus*. In response to some questions from Bernard Russell to a draft of the *Tractatus*, Wittgenstein writes that his 'main contention' is 'the theory of what can be expressed (*gesagt*) by propositions – i.e. by language – (and, which comes to the same, what can be *thought*) and what can not be expressed by prop[osition]s, but only shown (*gezeigt*)' (CL: 124), and he goes on to say that this is also, in his view, 'the cardinal problem of philosophy' (CL: 124; for discussion see Anscombe 1959: 161; Kremer 2007). This brings us to Wittgenstein's most important mention of the aim of the *Tractatus*, in its preface. This is important, not only because the preface has the textual authority of being Wittgenstein's most direct instrument in framing readers' approach to the *Tractatus*, but also because of his advice to von Ficker that attention to the preface is vital for an understanding of its ethical dimension. In the preface, Wittgenstein notes that 'the book deals with the problems of philosophy' (TLP: 3), and that he is confident to have found the solution to these problems but also that the *Tractatus* 'shows how little is achieved when these problems are solved' (TLP: 4). Furthermore, Wittgenstein again highlights the need to draw limits, now the limit of language, of 'the expression of thoughts' (TLP: 3), and he writes that the 'whole sense of the book might be summed up in the following words: what can be said at all can be said clearly, and of what we cannot talk we must pass over in silence' (TLP: 3; translation amended). This remark mirrors the very last sentence of the *Tractatus*: 'Of what we cannot speak we must pass over in silence' (TLP: 7; translation amended).

If we compare Wittgenstein's guides for reading, it becomes clear that they all present the *Tractatus* as revolving around a distinction between what can be said, and said clearly, and what cannot be said and not only has to be but also *ought to be* left in silence. Moreover, we learn a little more from each of the three guides, that this distinction sums up the 'sense of the book'; that ethics, as part of what cannot be expressed, can *only* be shown; that ethics is among what should be left in silence; and that in drawing attention to a connection between ethics and silence, Wittgenstein is trying to draw limits to the ethical 'from the inside', without assuming it possible to somehow see 'beyond' it (cf. CV: 22 [15]). These are Wittgenstein's suggested points of attention that we will take with us in the attempt to understand the role that ethics plays in the *Tractatus*.

2.2 The Remarks on Ethics

After having looked at Wittgenstein's guides for reading the *Tractatus*, it is time to turn to the remarks on ethics. These remarks are part of what I earlier singled out as part of the 'conclusion' of the *Tractatus*, the remarks from 6 onwards. We find the remarks on value in the 6.4s, and in the main sentence of this section, Wittgenstein writes that: 'All propositions [*Sätze*] are of equal value' (TLP 6.4). In the *Tractatus*, propositions or *Sätze* are meaningful sentences saying something about the world, and according to this remark, whatever we say about the world cannot stand out in terms of value. In the first commenting remark to 6.4, Wittgenstein elaborates on this point, writing: 'The sense of the world must lie outside the world. In the world everything is as it is, and everything happens as it does happen; *in it* no value exists – and if did exist, it would have no value' (TLP 6.41). On the picture of the world presented here, whatever happens *in* the world is a fact, and as such, it is contingent and does not matter in terms of value because value is something other than, and distinct from, contingency and facts. If we managed to find value in the world, it would also be contingent and thus not of value at all. Instead, Wittgenstein continues, value 'must lie outside the world' (TLP 6.41), connecting it to the sense or meaning of the world (TLP 6.41). As Iris Murdoch observes, it appears as if Wittgenstein is trying to avoid a devaluation of value by keeping it out of the world, 'to segregate value in order to keep it pure and untainted', separating 'the area of valueless contingency ... from the thereby purified ineffable activity of value'

(Murdoch 2003: 25 and 34). I think Murdoch's analysis is just right, and that one key to a satisfactory interpretation of ethics in the *Tractatus* is to reconstruct more specifically *how* Wittgenstein takes himself to be keeping value 'pure and untainted'.

The second line of commenting remarks after 6.4 is the only section where Wittgenstein uses the words 'ethics' and 'ethical', and I quote the main part of this section, as I return to it in this and following sections:

6.42   So too it is impossible for there to be propositions of ethics [*Sätze der Ethik*]. Propositions can express nothing that is higher.

6.421 It is clear that ethics cannot be put into words [*nicht aussprechen lässt*] Ethics is transcendental.

(Ethics and aesthetics are one and the same.)

6.422 When an ethical law of the form, 'Thou shalt . . .', is laid down, one's first thought is, 'And what if I do not do it?' It is clear, however, that ethics has nothing to do with punishment and reward in the usual sense of the terms. So our question about the *consequences* of an action must be unimportant. – At least those consequences should not be events. . . .

6.423 It is impossible to speak about the will as the bearer of the ethical [*Willen als dem Träger des Ethischen*]. And the will as a phenomenon is of interest only to psychology. (Translation amended)

Wittgenstein here introduces ethics as being in line with value and, in a similar way, tries to ascertain that ethics is not conflated with facts, even facts about consequences of actions or punishment and reward often considered central to ethics. That is, whatever Wittgenstein is doing, he is not presenting a run-of-the-mill understanding of ethics – ethics is not about right principles for action, good character or maximising the good, or anything else that is familiar or easily recognisable from the main traditions in moral philosophy. These traditions therefore cannot serve as a starting point of an interpretation of his remarks. In fact, when Wittgenstein writes that ethics cannot be put into words, he is presenting a view of ethics that, in Martin Stokhof's words, 'from the point of view of modern moral philosophy hardly deserves the name' (2002: 24).

Without any obvious frame of reference and struggling with the difficulty of trying to engage with a view of ethics that cannot be put into words, readers have found it difficult to work out a satisfactory interpretation of Tractarian ethics. This has led to a wealth of different readings, but one illuminating way to organise these readings is to divide them according to how they interpret Wittgenstein's point that there cannot be ethical sentences (TLP 6.42), and whether they connect this point to (1) Wittgenstein's view of what meaningful sentences can and cannot say, (2) his unusual, even radical view of philosophy in the *Tractatus*, or, finally, (3) the presentation of ethics as transcendental in a way parallel to logic. The first group of interpreters focuses on the idea that Wittgenstein in the *Tractatus* indicates or points to something specifically ethical while also insisting that this 'something' is not *in* the world, which means that it cannot be captured in meaningful sentences. They thus connect ethics to Wittgenstein's remark that the 'sense of the world ... must lie outside the world' (6.41), and their approach is by now often called *metaphysical*. In contrast to this, a second group of interpreters, now often called resolute readers, rejects the idea that the *Tractatus* specifies criteria for meaningful sentences. They rather think that Wittgenstein, in writing that 'ethics cannot be put into words', is working to show that silence is the right response to a proper understanding of the role that ethics plays into our life. The final group of readers finds a third starting point for interpretation in the parallels between the presentation of ethics and logic as transcendental in the *Tractatus*. This *logical* approach is, in my view, the most constructive way to approach ethics in the *Tractatus*. In the next chapter I will develop such a reading, but first, I present the two other approaches that have, until now, been most influential.

2.3 Metaphysical Approaches to Ethics

In the commentary literature on ethics in the *Tractatus*, there is a great variety of interpretations and a significant lack of consensus on most interpretative issues. I cannot discuss all interpretations but will present the two most influential approaches, the metaphysical and the resolute approaches just introduced. Both are concerned with the question of how to understand another of Wittgenstein's enigmatic guides for reading the *Tractatus*, when he, in its second to last remark, writes: 'My propositions serve as elucidations in the following way: anyone who understands me eventually recognizes them as nonsensical [*unsinnig*], when he has used them – as steps – to climb up beyond them' (TLP 6.54). In relation to these instructions, readers face a dilemma similar to that arising from the remarks on ethics: How are we to understand what Wittgenstein is doing in the *Tractatus*, if all of his sentences are in fact just plain nonsense and have no meaning for us to understand?

One of the earliest examples of a metaphysical approach can be found in Elizabeth Anscombe's seminal work *An Introduction to Wittgenstein's Tractatus* (1959). Anscombe wants to take seriously the idea that the sentences making up the *Tractatus* are nonsensical, while also acknowledging the importance that Wittgenstein places on such nonsense when produced by philosophical activity. Anscombe finds a way out of this conundrum by focusing on Wittgenstein's idea that 'What *can* be shown, *cannot* be said' (TLP 4.1212), also highlighted in the letter to von Ficker. She argues that even if 'attempts to say what is "shewn" produce "*non-sensical*" formations of words' (1959: 163), there is indeed 'something', some form of insight, that we can only approach through showing. On this view, the notion of showing is (among other things) meant to elucidate how nonsensical sentences can be used to point to 'truths' about the world that we cannot meaningfully say. In relation to these attempts to say what shows itself, Anscombe notes that 'it would be right to call them "true" if, *per impossibile*, they could be said; in fact they cannot be called true, since they cannot be said', continuing a little later: 'It would presumably be because of this that Wittgenstein regards the sentences of the *Tractatus* as helpful, in spite of their being strictly nonsensical according to the very doctrine that they propound' (1959: 162). According to Anscombe, philosophical and ethical 'sentences' are attempts to say what can only be shown that result in pseudo-truths and therefore are nonsensical.

Anscombe's idea of sentences indicating truths that cannot be said has been taken up by other interpreters, developing metaphysical approaches to the *Tractatus*. One such interpreter is Peter Hacker. He argues that Wittgenstein is trying to draw attention to a type of metaphysical 'insights' different from knowledge of facts, while at the same time thinking that 'sentences' presenting these 'insights' violate the rules of logical syntax, which means that attempts to express them result in a specific form of *illuminating* nonsense (cf. 2021: 18). Hacker thus develops a distinction between 'ordinary' meaningless sentences, which are plain nonsense, and a special type of meaningless sentences, which elucidate by 'showing' or 'pointing' to something outside of the world and outside language. Such illuminating, nonsensical sentences are unsuccessful attempts to express 'true' insights through illegitimate, sentence-like, but fundamentally meaningless linguistic constructions. In Hacker's words: 'What one *means* when one tries to state these insights is perfectly correct, but the endeavour must unavoidably fail. For the ineffable manifests itself, and cannot be said' (2000: 382). In a more recent defence of a metaphysical approach, Roger M. White presents the *Tractatus* as being 'concerned to specify precisely those features of reality that cannot be put into words and at the same time to bring out why they cannot be put into words' (2011: 22). Thus, central to metaphysical approaches is the idea that Wittgenstein in the *Tractatus* had to resort to illuminating nonsense to make readers aware of insights about the world that lie outside of language.

Metaphysical approaches to ethics share the ideas that the *Tractatus* presents a view of language that establishes a limit of meaning within which ethics cannot find a place, and that Wittgenstein uses the notion of showing to allow for the possibility that nonsensical sentences can still indicate insights related to ethics. Hacker also draws on this in his interpretation of ethics in the *Tractatus*, arguing that when Wittgenstein writes that ethics cannot be put into words, he is denying, not the existence of ethical insights or truths but rather that such 'truths' can be expressed in ordinary language because 'the philosophy of logic which [Wittgenstein] propounded drew the limits of language at the boundary of all that is "higher" – ethics, aesthetics, and religion, as well as philosophy itself' (2021: 105). According to Hacker, Wittgenstein's treatment of language, meaning, and logic in the *Tractatus* establishes an understanding of the limits of language according to which ethics falls outside the scope of what we can meaningfully say. David Wiggins also represents this approach, when he writes that 'Wittgenstein found himself driven to suppose that *some* kinds of apparent nonsense ... might *show* that which could not be said. Or, in the idiom I prefer, they might *point*' (2004: 385). Along similar lines, Allan Janik and Stephen Toulmin argue that Wittgenstein in the *Tractatus* wanted to present a general critique of language and use this critique to show '*both* that logic and science had a proper part to play within ordinary descriptive language ..., *and* that questions about "ethics, value and the meaning of life" by falling outside the limits of that descriptive language, become – at best – the object of a kind of mystical insight, which can be conveyed by "indirect" or poetical communication' (1973: 191; see also Collinson 1985: 270).

Among metaphysical readings, there are various suggestions for the kind of mystical insight indicated by the *Tractatus*. Hacker turns to entries from the *Notebooks* in 1916 to suggest that ethics, for Wittgenstein, is connected to a view of the subject that is inspired by Schopenhauer's concept of the transcendental ego. In the only remark mentioning Schopenhauer, Wittgenstein writes: 'It would be possible to say (à la Schopenhauer): It is not the world of Idea that is either good or evil; – but the willing subject ... not a part of the world but a presupposition of its existence' (NB: 79). Hacker connects this and related remarks to Tractarian remarks on 'the metaphysical subject, the limit of the world – not a part of it' (TLP 5.641) and on will as the bearer of ethics (6.423). He argues that Wittgenstein is presenting a doctrine termed by Hacker 'transcendental solipsism' that concerns the metaphysical self as 'the constant form of all experience' (Hacker 2021: 103) and involves a number of 'obscure theories about ethics, the will, aesthetics, and religion' (100). According to Hacker, the insights or theories connected to transcendental solipsism cannot be said but Wittgenstein thought them to be evident because all other propositions 'manifest the transcendental truths that cannot be said' (104).

A related, and somewhat more enthusiastic, reading of Tractarian ethics as inspired by fundamental Schopenhauerian insights is developed by Martin

Stokhof, who also sees Wittgenstein as attempting to convey insights into the metaphysical subject as a condition of, among other things, ethics (see 2002: 191–6). Central to Hacker's and Stokhof's readings of Tractarian ethics is the focus on special ethical insights that cannot refer to the world but must instead allude to something at the limit of the world. Stokhof even says that ethics must be placed *outside* the world, as 'both value and its expression belong to another realm' (2002: 212), which could be interpreted as, in Wittgenstein's terms, an attempt to see beyond the limit of language. In general, metaphysical approaches consider ethical and mystical insights as somehow placed 'beside' the world of facts and language, finding in the *Tractatus* an expression of 'the feeling that the world is not everything, that there is something outside it' (Ramsey 1923: 478).

There are at least three challenges facing metaphysical approaches to ethics. The first concerns the idea that ethics involves insights pointing to something that cannot find a place in the world but is somehow placed 'outside' of it. This amounts to a reading of ethics as *transcendent*, and it finds some support in Wittgenstein's remark that the 'sense of the world must lie outside of the world' (TLP 6.41), but it conflicts with the presentation of ethics as 'transcendental' (TLP 6.421), that is, *not* as somehow beyond the realm of the real but as part of what conditions engagement with the real. Several observations support the idea that Wittgenstein upholds this distinction between transcendent and transcendental. His use of 'transcendental' in relation to ethics reflects a central remark earlier in the *Tractatus*, stating that 'Logic is transcendental' (TLP 6.13). This shows that the roles played by logic and ethics are at least in some respects parallel, but it is much harder to make a case for the idea that logic (and not just ethics) should be seen as transcendent, placed somehow *outside* the world. Moreover, the idea that the *Tractatus* involves metaphysical insights about ethics also seems to be in tension with the preface of the book. Wittgenstein writes here that he has found the solution to the problems of philosophy, but he could hardly have stated this with such confidence if he saw the *Tractatus* as presenting transcendent insights representing 'an exotic variety of metaphysics that generates new philosophical problems' (Engelmann 2021: 8).

The second challenge, relevant to only some metaphysical readings, is exegetical and concerns the claim that ethics in the *Tractatus* is somehow influenced by Schopenhauer. This relies heavily on remarks from the *Notebooks*, most of which do not appear in the *Tractatus*, making it hard to assess whether Wittgenstein held on to the more Schopenhauerian ideas considered in the summer of 1916 (see Tejedor 2010: 90–1, for an overview of textual connections between *Notebooks* and *Tractatus*). The final challenge facing metaphysical approaches is not exegetic, but general, and it concerns the attempt to hold a view according to which nonsensical sentences are devoid of meaning but may still (in some way or other) be used to show or point to fundamentally inexpressible insights. Critics object that metaphysical readers try to hold two incompatible claims: that meaningless sentences are just plain nonsense, and that some forms of nonsense may still have some kind of 'meaning' conveying 'insights'. When trying to understand *Tractatus* 6.54, metaphysical readers are, in Cora Diamond's delightful phrase, 'chickening out' (1988: 181). They waver irresolutely between two different understanding of nonsense, unable to accept that nonsensical sentences are characterised precisely by saying nothing at all, and that Wittgenstein's sentences in the main bulk of the *Tractatus* therefore are just plain nonsense (cf. TLP: 6.54, see e.g. Conant and Diamond 2004; Conant and Bronzo 2017: 180–1).

2.4 Resolute Approaches to Ethics

A rival to the metaphysical approach is the resolute approach, which is primarily concerned with interpretating Wittgenstein's 'guide' for understanding in *Tractatus* 6.54. The resolute approach covers many different readings and is more a framework for understanding the *Tractatus* than a full interpretation, even if the shared origin of resolute readings makes them somewhat more aligned than metaphysical ones (see e.g. Read and Deans 2003; Conant and Diamond 2004; Kuusela 2011). Resolute readers agree that when Wittgenstein writes that his sentences in the *Tractatus* should be recognised 'as nonsensical' (6.54), we should accept this description and see his sentences as exactly that, just plain nonsense. When engaging with the *Tractatus*, readers should not attribute to Wittgenstein the contradictory endeavour of attempting to alert us to metaphysical but ineffable 'insights' or 'doctrines' while claiming that these cannot be said; instead readers should, *resolutely* as it were, accept 'that the elucidatory sentences of the *Tractatus* must ultimately be recognized as *simply* nonsensical, i.e., as forms of words that neither say nor quasi-say anything' (Conant and Bronzo 2017: 176). It is a form of confusion to attempt to quasi-talk or use nonsense to point to insights, and when Wittgenstein distinguishes between saying and showing, he takes showing to apply *only* to meaningful sentences, not to irresolute attempts to hint at some form of 'content' that really cannot be said (cf. Conant 2005: 67).

Resolute readers also agree that whatever strings of language are to be identified as meaningful or nonsensical depends, not on applying some specialised Tractarian doctrines specifying criteria for meaningful language, but rather on the capacities involved in ordinary ways of speaking and thinking (Conant 2005; Conant and Bronzo 2017). In a presentation of the core assumptions of resolute readings, Cora Diamond and James Conant emphasise that this non-theorical understanding of meaning also applies to the philosophical method of logical clarification adopted by Wittgenstein in the *Tractatus* (see TLP 4.112). That is, Wittgenstein 'did not take the procedure of clarification, as he then conceived it, to depend on anything more than the logical capacities that are part of speaking and thinking' (Conant and Diamond 2004: 64).

By simply accepting Wittgenstein's own description of Tractarian sentences as nonsense, resolute readers avoid the uncomfortable idea that he tries to indicate some 'insight' with his uses of words, but they instead face the challenge of having to give an alternative answer to the question of what his purpose could be in producing the intricate nonsense presented in the *Tractatus*. Diamond and Conant emphasise that an answer to this question can be developed differently by different resolute readers, but that it will be an answer according to which the nonsensical sentences of the *Tractatus* offer the reader the possibility of engaging with claims that philosophers may *want* to come to make but that philosophers also, as they work through these apparent claims, come to recognise as really not claims at all. By engaging with the *Tractatus*, readers come to realise that 'the very questions that we are initially inclined to take [Wittgenstein] to be addressing are themselves not questions at all' (Conant and Diamond 2004: 64). Wittgenstein is not trying to make us show or point to what we cannot say but nevertheless claim is true; he is rather trying to bring us to realise that our attempts to show or indicate something that cannot be expressed are just empty gestures, thus enabling us to give up these attempts. The nonsense making up the *Tractatus* offers a therapeutic journey that reveals to readers the paradox involved in something like the metaphysical approach.

If we accept the resolute rejection of the possibility of metaphysical nonsense, this allows us to turn to a different question, namely why we are so easily tempted by the idea of quasi-saying something that we cannot straightforwardly express. One possible answer is that this temptation arises because we are undecided about what we want to say while still wanting to insist that there is some insight hidden in our unsettled attempts to talk. Cora Diamond points to this tendency of projecting our own undecidedness onto the possibilities of language: 'We are so convinced that we understand what we are trying to say that we see only the two possibilities: *it* is sayable, *it* is not sayable. But Wittgenstein's aim is to allow us to see that there is no "it"' (Diamond 1988: 198). Through engagement with the kind of nonsense making up the *Tractatus*, we come to realise that our attempts to show something that cannot be said are futile because they are *indeterminate*; because 'there is no coherent understanding to be reached of what [we] wanted to say' (Diamond 1988: 198). The idea of 'the ineffable' becomes attractive because we cannot make up our mind about what we want to say, and the way to come to give up this idea is by realising that the problems we have with expressing ourselves are not produced by some inability of language but rather by our own indecisiveness.

There are at least two ways of understanding Wittgenstein's method of using nonsense as a means of elucidation in the *Tractatus*, which I will term strong and mild resolutism respectively (cf. Kuusela 2011). Strong resolutist readers hold that Tractarian elucidation always proceeds in a *piecemeal way*, addressing specific philosophical problems or confusions with the linguistic methods needed in that specific case (cf. Read and Deans 2003). This exclusively piecemeal approach rejects the idea that the *Tractatus* offers a general method of clarification, and because of this, it rules out the possibility of general logical achievements of the *Tractatus* (cf. Kuusela 2011: 127). It thus has difficulties explaining why Wittgenstein thought the *Tractatus* offers a method of clarification that can address and solve all 'the problems of philosophy' (TLP: 3).

These problems have made *mild* resolute readers suggest that the discussion of logic in the *Tractatus* is intended to culminate in a general method of philosophical clarification that revolves around the logical analysis of the general proposition. On this view, Wittgenstein is trying to develop 'an allegedly universally applicable method of logical analysis that embodies a conception of *the* essence of propositions . . . and is intended to be universally applicable in the clarification of any logical unclarity' (Kuusela 2011: 132). Instead of presenting criteria of meaning (as assumed by metaphysical readers), the discussion of logic in the *Tractatus* is intended to establish a *general* philosophical method. Relatedly, Cora Diamond notes that the *Tractatus* 'is metaphysical in holding that the logical relations of our thoughts to each other can be shown, completely shown, in an analysis of our propositions. . . . What is metaphysical is not the content of some belief, but the laying down of requirement, the requirement of logical analysis' (1991: 18–19). Mild resolutist interpretations of logical clarification thus see the *Tractatus* as Wittgenstein's attempt to set up a general framework for logical analysis of philosophical nonsense – a general, logical method of elucidation.

Common for resolute readings of ethics in the *Tractatus* is that they can acknowledge the connection that Wittgenstein establishes between ethics and silence in his various guides for reading. Resolute readers hold that the main achievement of the *Tractatus* is to make us realise that our attempts to talk about metaphysical or ineffable 'insights' are misguided because the questions we take ourselves to be addressing are not really questions at all, and they thus give substance to the idea that engagement with Wittgenstein's work should end in silence. Furthermore, as this achievement is brought about through a change in our relation to our words and in what we expect of them, reading the *Tractatus* does seem to have an integral ethical dimension – its ultimate aim is a transformation of the reader. As James Conant writes:

> reaping the ethical teaching of the book would consist not in one's having learnt something from *what it says* about matters (about which one thinks one wants to learn), but rather in one's having allowed the work to transform one's conception of what it is that one really wants (from a book about philosophy or logic or ethics) – where this, in turn, requires a transformation of one's self. (2005: 46)

For resolute readers, the ethical aim of the *Tractatus* is to draw a limit to language (as Wittgenstein writes to von Ficker) by making the reader give up metaphysical aspirations and come to recognise ways of making sense that are already available with their everyday mastery of language.

In his resolute reading of ethics in the *Tractatus*, Michael Kremer argues that Wittgenstein is concerned to deflect deeply rooted but ultimately misguided needs for absolute justifications, also in relation to our ethical lives. When Wittgenstein in 6.422 writes that our first reaction to an ethical law is 'And what if I do not do it?' (TLP 6.422), he shows us that if something can be established as a definitive justification in ethics, it can also be contested, and if we develop this line of thought, we come to realise that whatever may be intelligibly asserted as an ethical justification may also be intelligibly denied. The right response to the need for ethical justification is to realise that this need does not have an 'answer' because really there is no 'question'. In relation to value and ethics: 'The *riddle* does not exist' (TLP 6.5). Wittgenstein's aim is that this realisation can bring about a form of ethical conversion that frees the reader from the conflicted and confused motivations leading to the need for ultimate justifications. In this way, Kremer claims, engagement with the *Tractatus* gives us 'knowledge-how' and enables us to turn to the real task of living our lives: 'To understand this book and its author is to learn how to live. The book *shows* us how to live, but does not *tell* us this' (2001: 62, cf. 58, 61).

Resolute readings of Tractarian ethics have many merits. They align with Wittgenstein's guides for reading and the description of his remarks as non-sense, just as they can make sense of the aim to draw limits to ethics and language from the inside and to respond to ethics with silence. Still, these readings face a challenge that connects with the way that Conant and Kremer, in presenting the aim of the *Tractatus*, move from philosophical to ethical and existential problems. They both start with Wittgenstein addressing a reader in the grip of philosophical illusions, but they move from there to Wittgenstein addressing a reader engaged in existential challenges, facing everyone, of how to transform oneself or live rightly. This is problematic because Wittgenstein never presents the *Tractatus* as offering practical ethical guidance. In the preface, he says clearly that his 'book deals with the problems of philosophy' (TLP: 3) and that the value it may have consists in showing 'how little has been done when these problems have been solved' (TLP: 3). This is not a presentation of a book providing a guide for living, and it indicates that we should look for an interpretation according to which the *Tractatus* is addressing, not existential, but specifically *philosophical* confusions about ethics.

There is, or so I am arguing, more work to be done in order to unfold the specific forms of philosophical confusions about ethics that Wittgenstein is addressing. Strong resolute readers may see no need to do this, as elucidation is piecemeal and the philosophical confusions about ethics addressed by Wittgenstein may be quite different from those haunting us now. But mild resolutist readers, by assuming that the *Tractatus* presents a general method of elucidation, seem obliged to address the question of *what kind* of philosophical therapy that Wittgenstein is offering in relation to ethics in the *Tractatus*. This is the question to which I turn in the next chapter.

3 The *Tractatus* Remarks on Ethics Again: A Reading

3.1 Ethical Silence Re-visited (TLP 6.42)

In the last chapter, I introduced the remarks on ethics in the *Tractatus* together with two influential approaches to these remarks. In this chapter, I present the reading that I find best does justice to Wittgenstein's text. I do so by reading the remarks on ethics slowly (cf. CV: 65 [57]), focusing on one remark at a time.

Any investigation of the remarks on ethics must, of course, take into account Wittgenstein's presentation of his philosophical method in the *Tractatus* as 'the logical clarification of thoughts ... not a body of doctrine but an activity', as well as his idea that a philosophical work consists 'essentially of elucidations' and results in 'the logical clarification of thoughts' (TLP 4.112). In my view, Wittgenstein sees logical clarification as elucidations of conditions of language that can be appreciated by reflecting on ordinary uses of words, in line with the understanding of elucidation developed in Marie McGinn's logical interpretation of the *Tractatus*, where its philosophical method is understood as anti-metaphysical while still 'aiming to present positive philosophical insights into the nature of language' (2006: 6). McGinn thinks that we can best substantiate Wittgenstein's claim to have provided 'the final solutions of the problems' (TLP: 4) of philosophy by connecting it to the assumption that he in the *Tractatus* delivers a general method of elucidation that can be applied to *any* philosophical problem and solve it permanently, more specifically, the assumption that 'once the nature of a proposition has become clear, then everything will be clear' (McGinn 2006: 15–16). My approach is thus also related to mild resolutism by acknowledging that Wittgenstein's sentences in the *Tractatus* 'serve as elucidations' and are 'nonsensical' (TLP 6.54), and that he also wants the work to establish a general method of elucidation 'once and for all and in advance of the latter's employments in particular cases' (Kuusela 2011: 132).

In my view, an important background for any reading of ethics in the *Tractatus* is the strikingly untraditional conception of ethics that appears more generally in Wittgenstein's early writings. As noted earlier, his engagement with issues of value opens with an entry in the *Notebooks* in 1916 on God and the purpose of life (NB: 72). Ethics is introduced some ten days later, when Wittgenstein connects it to will and notes that a world without will would also be 'a world without ethics' (NB: 77). The section on ethics in the *Tractatus*, 6.4n, also includes writings on value (TLP 6.4), the 'sense of the world' (TLP 6.41), 'the limits of the world' (TLP 6.43), and 'the mystical' (TLP 6.44). Ethics is presented as 'transcendental' (TLP 6.421; cf. NB: 79) and is again connected to will (TLP 6.423; NB: 77, 80) together with questions of aesthetics (TLP 6.421; NB: 77, 83; LE: 38) and God (TLP 6.432; NB: 72–9; LE: 42; CV: 5 [3]). Almost all of these ways of characterising ethics are in play in 'A Lecture on Ethics', where Wittgenstein first presents the definition that 'Ethics is the general enquiry into what is good' (LE: 38), before he goes on to say that he will 'use the term Ethics in a slightly wider sense' (LE: 38) than is customary in moral philosophy. Wittgenstein then presents his listeners with a row of synonyms that he hopes will suggest to them a rough idea of what he finds are the characteristic features of ethics: 'Ethics is the enquiry into what is valuable, or, into what is really important, or I could have said Ethics is the enquiry into the meaning of life, or into what makes life worth living, or into the right way of living' (LE: 38). At the end of the lecture, Wittgenstein adds that ethics springs from the need to address 'the ultimate meaning of life, the absolute good, the absolute valuable' (LE: 44).

Held together, Wittgenstein's various characterisations reveal a view of ethics that is very broad but revolves around a connection between subject and will, on the one hand, and life and world, on the other hand, as Wittgenstein brings into play notions of the sense of the world as well as the meaning, value, and problem(s) in life. Ethics concerns a subject's relation to their life and the world in which this life is situated, and by including the will in this cluster of characterisations, Wittgenstein also highlights that this subject is, at least potentially, active. By drawing connections between ethics, questions of value and meaning, and the task of having a life to lead, many of the questions that Wittgenstein relates to ethics are closer to what academic philosophers today would call questions of the meaning of life than to questions normally assumed to be part of moral philosophy, such as questions concerning principles of right and wrong action, good or bad character, or the consequences of our actions. Wittgenstein's inclusive understanding of ethics also goes some way to explain why he connects ethics to questions about aesthetics and God, which are often also considered central to the question of how to live a meaningful life.

One remark that deserves special attention is when Wittgenstein in 'A Lecture on Ethics' says that ethics is the 'enquiry into' what is valuable and so on. Wittgenstein does not identify ethics with what is valuable and so on; rather, he identifies ethics with attempts to examine or investigate value and morality, as we, for example, find them in philosophy. This is a significant point, and it can help us understand Wittgenstein's perhaps most striking characterisation of ethics, when he in 'A Lecture on Ethics' says that engaging with ethics is 'to run against the boundaries of language', a hopeless 'running against the walls of our cage' (LE: 44). Wittgenstein here seems to paint a rather bleak picture of moral engagement, as hopeless inexpressibility, but there is room for caution because it is, importantly, *enquiries* into the meaning and value of life, such as *philosophical* enquiries, that Wittgenstein describes as running against the limits of language, not the practical, everyday endeavour of engaging in moral life. Wittgenstein insists on silence in ethics in his philosophical work and in discussions with philosophers, and what he criticises as hopeless is not the attempt to live a life with meaning and value, but the ideas that moral life can meaningfully be a subject of philosophy, and that we can enquire into why and how such a life is possible (cf. Cahill 2004: 49). As Wittgenstein told a friend after finishing the manuscript for the *Tractatus*, 'The question is solved: *philosophy* is silencing, the remainder is doing, [which] means: becoming a decent person' (Hänsel 2012: 51, emphases added; quoted from Engelmann 2021: 66). In line with this, I argue that we should also read the remarks on ethics in the *Tractatus* to address *philosophical* confusions about ethics and read Wittgenstein's pleas for silence as pleas for philosophical silence about ethics.

When engaging with ethics in the *Tractatus*, we thus need to remember that Wittgenstein is engaging with us as philosophers. With this in mind, I return to the first remark on ethics that 'it is impossible for there to be propositions of ethics' (TLP 6.42) and the way it connects to Wittgenstein's pleas for silence in ethics. In my view, this remark thus addresses attempts to state philosophical insights about ethics – what philosophers think they can say about what has to be in place for there to be questions of right and wrong, good or bad, and so on. Wittgenstein is simply taking it for granted that having a life to live is to engage with questions of meaning and value, and what he wants to challenge, and dissolve, is what he sees as certain philosophical confusions about what can be said about the background of such activities. He thus criticises the inclination to try to explicate, explain, and justify the conditions of the possibility of moral life, not moral life itself.

It is possible to bring out how this difference between philosophising and living influences Wittgenstein's remarks on ethics by turning to a question not yet considered in any depth: what does Wittgenstein mean by 'propositions of ethics'? As we saw, metaphysical readers assume that if there are no ethical sentences, then any form of ethically relevant talk will result in nonsense. However, this is not what Wittgenstein writes in the *Tractatus*. He writes that his own elucidations should be recognised 'as nonsensical' (TLP 6.54), but in relation to ethics, he simply says that it 'cannot be put into words' (TLP 6.421) and is 'impossible to speak about' (TLP 6.423). As we have now come to see, these warnings concern *enquiries into* the conditions of ethics. To put it bluntly, it is *philosophical* enquires into ethics that result in nonsensical sentences. Furthermore, an important insight motivating the resolute approach is that investigations into whether a sentence has meaning or not are to be decided simply by using the capacities involved in ordinary language, as Wittgenstein also reminds us by writing in the preface that the 'whole sense' of the *Tractatus* is that 'what can be said at all can be said clearly' (TLP: 3). The aim of the *Tractatus* is not to exclude, as nonsensical, ordinary uses of language that are straightforwardly meaningful for speakers in everyday circumstances, and this point of course also applies to ordinary uses of language that concern ethics and value.

I will bring out this point by introducing an example. Let us imagine a situation where I say to a friend that she was wrong not to tell her young child about the death of a distant cousin, and she responds that even if she did tell her son a lie, this was the right thing to do because right now, her son is psychologically frail and worried about the finitude of life and the possibility of death in a way that makes him unable to handle the truth. However, she will of course tell him later when there is no risk that the news of the death of her cousin will feed into her son's general anxieties or shake his trust in life. In this situation, when using our ordinary linguistic capacities, my friend and I have no trouble understanding the meaning of our sentences – in fact, no questions of the meaning of these sentences arise for us, and we would respond with bewilderment if someone was to suggest that our sentences were nonsensical or aiming to say something that cannot be put into words. That is, even if some of our sentences could be labelled 'ethical (or moral) propositions', sentences like these cannot be what Wittgenstein rules out in the *Tractatus*.

When Wittgenstein rejects the possibility of ethical propositions, he cannot be thinking of ordinary exchanges of moral relevance. That is, he cannot be ruling out the numerous perfectly meaningful exchanges that ordinary speakers have about what is right and wrong, good or bad, virtuous or wicked or about how to establish meaning and value in life, because these sentences obviously have meaning in quite ordinary uses of language. Wittgenstein in fact makes it quite clear that he is not trying to rule out such ordinary talk, including talk of something as valuable or meaningful, writing that 'all the propositions of our everyday language, just as they stand, are in perfect logical order' (TLP 5.5563). Wittgenstein must be elucidating another set of difficulties, and my suggestion is that these difficulties concern philosophical attempts to explicate *how* life and the world can come to have meaning, or in more Tractarian terms, to explicate or say the conditions of ethics or express what 'is higher' (TLP 6.42). Returning to Wittgenstein's reading guides, it is now clear that in relation to ethics, the distinction between what can be said and what cannot be said and ought to be left in silence is a distinction between ordinary ways of talking about and dealing with value and meaning in life, on the one hand, and (philosophical) attempts to say what makes such dealings *possible*, on the other. The ethical silence recommended by Wittgenstein is the right response to the latter but not the former set of activities. It is impossible for there to be philosophical propositions of ethics (cf. TLP 6.42).

3.2 Logic and Ethics Are Transcendental (TLP 6.421)

I now turn to the remarks commenting on 6.42. However, to clarify these remarks, I will go beyond Wittgenstein's 'guide' to von Ficker – that an understanding of the ethical importance of the *Tractatus* could be developed by reading 'the *preface* and the *conclusion*' (EN: 144) – because the section that introduces value and ethics, from 6.4 and onwards, revolves around a number of words – will, world, life, and transcendental – which also appear earlier in the *Tractatus*. This gives me reason to look at these earlier appearances to consider how they connect to the remarks on ethics.

The *Tractatus* opens by introducing a notion of 'world': 'The world is all that is the case' (TLP 1). This opening has sometimes been interpreted as an ontological claim on Wittgenstein's part, about what does and does not exist, but if we take seriously that the *Tractatus* is offering elucidations, not metaphysics, the remark must play another role. The most striking feature of the remark is that it is, in a sense, devoid of information, almost like an entry in a dictionary, simply explicating the meaning of 'the world' as the word we use to talk about everything there is. Looked at in this way, Wittgenstein is not making a substantial claim but is simply illuminating how we use the word 'world' to talk of all there is. Moreover, as the world is 'all that is the case', everything that there is, this implies that if something exists, it is (necessarily or a priori) *in* the world. In this way, the remark reminds us of how we use the word 'world' and provides 'logical clarification' (TLP 4.112).

If we consider only the first remark of the *Tractatus*, the world may appear simply as a grouping, assemblage, or heap of something, but in order for us to talk about *the* world, the world must have some form of unity or organisation. This clarification is offered in the very next sentence, when Wittgenstein writes that the 'world is the totality of facts, not of things' (TLP 1.1). Facts are more than just heaps of things; for us to talk of facts, they have to be unities with some form of formal organisation, and this point equally applies to talk of the world, which must also have some form of formal organisation. Wittgenstein brings out this feature of talk about the world and facts, writing that the 'facts in logical space are the world' (TLP 1.13). The world is a unity because it consists of facts organised in logical space, and facts are separate unities because they take up a specific place in logical space. Again, as Wittgenstein is only providing elucidations, this is not a substantial or metaphysical claim about the organisation of reality but rather a clarification of what has to be in place for us to talk or think about something as a fact or the world – what is logically necessary.

According to the Wittgenstein of the *Tractatus*, we do not have to make specific discoveries to see that our ability to talk or think about the world is dependent on the world being organised in a way that is available for language and thought. Rather, the logical organisation of the world is something that can be clarified independently of any actual understanding of or discovery about the world. Logic is not dependent on the existence of specific facts or a specific world; rather, it is connected to the very fact that something (anything) exists – something that we can represent in language. 'The "experience" that we need in order to understand logic is not that something or other is the state of things, but that something *is*: that, however, is *not* an experience', Wittgenstein writes, adding, '[l]ogic is *prior* to every experience – that something *is so*' (TLP 5.552). It is no accident that logic applies to the world because logic is a condition of the possibility of talking about the world, and because of this, logic cannot itself be a fact in the world (cf. TLP 5.5521). As Marie McGinn writes, 'Wittgenstein's idea is that we can understand how logic applies to the world only if the world and logic are reciprocal notions: there is no representation of the world without logic and there is no logic without representation of the world' (2006: 244). World and logic are mutually dependent notions, neither of which is possible without the other.

In the same way, it is no accident that logic applies to language. In any meaningful uses of language, we rely on the whole of logic because a sentence can only show its specific sense if the force of the sentence 'reaches through the whole of logical space' (TLP 3.42). A meaningful sentence shows its meaning: what would be the case in the world if the sentence is true, the facts we would find there, and the sentence says that this is actually the case (TLP 4.022).

In doing so, the sentence also shows the logical form of the world, which is the necessary condition for saying that anything is true (TLP 4.121). Logic shows what is essential to the activity of engaging in meaningful language, and in this way, our language use shows logic, but we cannot make logic the subject of this use. 'Propositions cannot represent logical form: it is mirrored in them. What finds its reflection in language, language cannot represent. ... Propositions *show* the logical form of reality' (TLP 4.121). Here, we again encounter what Wittgenstein, in his letter to Russell, calls the cardinal problem of philosophy, the distinction between 'what can be expressed by propositions . . . and what can not be expressed by prop[osition]s, but only shown' (CL: 124). In any particular instance of language use, we draw on the whole of logic, which means that we should see logic as a formal condition of language that cannot itself be expressed in language. 'What *can* be shown, *cannot* be said' (TLP 4.1212). As the structure of the activity of representation, logic cannot itself be represented; we cannot say or quasi-say logic; rather, logic shows as the condition of whatever we choose to say.

Logic cannot be said and cannot be described in language because it is completely uninformative and empty of content. Thus, there are no logical doctrines or logical *Lehre*; rather, logic shows itself as the shared organisation of world and language reflected in any instance of language use. For us to be able to use language to talk about the world, we draw on what is common for both, and this is logic: 'Logic pervades the world: the limits of the world are also its limits' (TLP 5.61). Logic is neither in nor outside the world, neither factual nor transcendent; instead, logic is what conditions our engagement with the world in language. In this sense, logic is given a priori (TLP 5.473; cf. Engelmann 2021: 55–6), and what is a priori cannot be factual, as Wittgenstein notes, because all 'we see could be other than it is. ... There is no a priori order of things' (TLP 5.634). In general, this is what shows itself: the a priori and necessary but formal and empty conditions for the representation of the world in language and thought.

When Wittgenstein says that the relation between what we can say and what only shows itself is his 'main contention' and 'the cardinal problem of philosophy' (CL: 124), he is presenting a view of philosophy concerned with what is known a priori, but that is, as such, purely formal and empty of content. Moreover, when he in *Tractatus* 6 introduces 'the general form of propositions' (TLP 6, translation amended), this indicates his main aim of presenting a general elucidation of logic is completed. This opens the question of what Wittgenstein is doing in the following remarks – what I, in section 2.1, identified as the 'conclusion' of the *Tractatus* – and I adopt Engelmann's suggestion that Wittgenstein here moves on to handle 'various philosophical problems ... in a sequence of subjects according to kinds of Satz: logic (6.1n), mathematics (6.2n), science (6.3n), ethics and value (6.4n), and the riddle of life (6.5n)' (2021: 54). Running through this treatment of philosophical problems is the aim of elucidating the distinction between what concerns the facts and is accidental but informative and what concerns the a priori and is necessary but uninformative and only shows itself. Wittgenstein's rejection of the idea of a priori *truths* has important implications for philosophy. In his view, philosophy is concerned with necessary conditions for world and language, and when these cannot be said, it follows that philosophy has no independent field of study, and that there are no philosophical sentences. Instead, philosophy clarifies the formal conditions of representation and is, in this way, inextricably linked to the difference between what can be said and what can only be shown.

In the first set of remarks on philosophical problems of logic (6.1n), Wittgenstein writes that the 'propositions of logic are tautologies' (TLP 6.1) and continues '[t]herefore the propositions of logic say nothing' (TLP 6.11). Wittgenstein here opposes the idea, prominent in the work of Bertrand Russell and Gottlob Frege, that logic is a special group of necessary truths, because if logic is purely formal and uninformative, it does not have any content and thus can be neither true nor false. In fact, Wittgenstein calls this his 'fundamental idea' that 'there can be no representatives of the *logic* of facts' (TLP 4.0312). In elucidating logic, we learn nothing about the world; that is, we learn nothing at all. 'Logic is not a body of doctrine, but a mirror-image of the world. Logic is transcendental' (TLP 6.13). Wittgenstein thus uses the word 'transcendental' to signal that logic is a necessary condition of language, which is reflected in meaningful uses of sentences but does not have content and cannot be talked about. This is the reason why the 'correct method in philosophy would really be . . . to say nothing except what can be said . . . i.e. something that has nothing to do with philosophy' (TLP 6.53) and why the sentences of the *Tractatus* really are 'nonsensical' (TLP 6.54).

With this in mind, I return to the second remark on ethics in the *Tractatus*, stating 'It is clear that ethics cannot be put into words. Ethics is transcendental' (TLP 6.421), to explore the connection between the presentation of ethics and logic as transcendental (cf. TLP 6.13). Wittgenstein shows how logic, as the necessary condition of representation, does not connect to specific facts but to how 'something *is*' (TLP 5.552), just as he remarks that in the world 'no value exists' (TLP 6.41), that value and ethics do not connect to specific facts, '*how* things are in the world', but to '*that* it exists' (TLP 6.44). Logic and ethics are similar insofar as they do not concern facts and cannot be represented in language, and when ethics is presented as transcendental, just like logic, this means that ethics is also (in some way or other) a formal condition of having a world. As transcendental, ethics must, like logic, concern the way the world have to be organised in order to be a world, making it a priori and empty of content.

There is, however, one notable difference between logic and ethics. While there are no propositions of ethics, there is indeed a special form of propositions of logic, tautologies. Tautologies have 'a unique status among all propositions' (TLP 6.112) because they say *nothing* (TLP 5.43, 6.11) and rather represent 'the scaffolding of the world' (TLP 6.124) or the 'logic of the world' (TLP 6.22). This difference arises because logic is connected to the possibility of representation, while ethics must concern some other aspect of our relationship to the world. Drawing on Wittgenstein's broad view of ethics and the preceding remark, 6.41, stating that value and meaning cannot be in in the world, the best suggestion is that ethics is concerned with the possibility of organising the world in terms of meaning and value. As Kristen Boyce notes, saying that logic is transcendental is 'to say that it is a virtue of logic . . . that our thinking hangs together across different contexts in describing a world. To say that ethics and aesthetics, too, are transcendental is to say that it is not solely in virtue of a concern for truth that that our thinking transcends individual contexts and hangs together' (2019: 139–40). Organisation in terms of value and meaning is part of what constitutes a world because without it, a world could not be a world *for someone* – a point I return to in the next section.

This view of ethics as a condition of the organisation of the world in terms of value can be elaborated on by comparing it with what Wittgenstein writes about science in the *Tractatus* – also in the concluding section on philosophical problems. In the set of remarks beginning with 6.3, Wittgenstein elucidates the difference between law and accident, necessity and contingency, bringing out how the various 'laws' of the natural sciences show themselves as a priori because they determine the specific ways of describing the world that constitute the natural sciences in the way that mechanics, for example, conditions a very specific form of description – that of attempting to 'construct according to a single plan all the *true* propositions that we need for the description of the world' (TLP 6.343). As conditions of specific forms of descriptions of the world, the fundamental laws of natural science are a priori and necessary, but they are also not about facts and cannot be described in language. In a metaphor offered by Wittgenstein, if the sciences are like various forms of nets used to describe reality, a scientific law concerns the type of net used, not the facts, 'what the net describes' (TLP 6.35). To take one example, the notion of a law of causality does not reflect some necessary fact about the world; rather, it presents itself as a necessary condition of a scientific organisation of the world, and as such, it 'cannot be said: it shows itself' (TLP 6.36, translation amended).

However, even if we cannot express the 'law' of causality, this does not mean that we should stop talking in science; rather, in presenting scientific sentences (that may turn out to be true or false according to the quality of our scientific engagement), the 'law' of causality will show itself.

This is an important similarity between science and ethics. In the same way, even if we cannot say or express ethics, this does not mean that we should stop talking in moral life because when we talk about what we find right or wrong, valuable or meaningful, ethics will show itself as the organisation of these ways of talking. As long as we do not take the a priori conditions of the laws of science or ethics to be 'about' some special sort of 'facts' (in or outside the world), such as for example 'facts' of causality or value, and we do not try to express or talk about these conditions, to say what ethics *is* for example, we are not sentenced to silence (as brought out in the previous example of the discussion between me and my friend). Still, Wittgenstein points to an important difference between science and ethics by presenting ethics as transcendental, without presenting science in the same way. In relation to science, we are free either to engage in scientific investigations of the world or to refrain from doing so. In this way, science is simply one system among others with which we can approach the world, a 'modern system' (TLP 6.372), as Wittgenstein writes, akin to older systems of God and fate. We do *not*, however, have the same freedom in relation to ethics. When ethics is presented as transcendental this indicates that we cannot choose whether or not to engage with value. Rather, having a world necessarily means to relate to the world in terms of meaning and value, that is, to engage in ethics. Why this is so will be the topic of the next section.

3.3 World and 'I', Will and Ethics (TLP 6.423)

In the *Tractatus*, Wittgenstein shows how for something to be the world, it has to be organised in a way that is available for language and thought, and that logic, as this form of organisation, is transcendental and cannot itself be expressed in language. Wittgenstein also shows how ethics plays a similar role, and that ethics, as the possibility of organising the world in terms of meaning and value, is transcendental and cannot itself be expressed in language. Logic and ethics are, however, not the only necessary conditions of a notion of the world. For something to be the world, it also has to be the world *for* someone because only with the introduction of an 'I' that can think and talk about the world does the world appear as a unity that is available in language and thought. In this way, the '*limits of my language* mean the limits of my world' (TLP 5.6). What brings the subject into philosophy is that the world only comes into view from a specific perspective, for an 'I', and the 'I' is, in this specific sense, nothing more than a perspective on the world. The 'I' and the world are mutually constitutive so that, really, the 'world is *my* world' (TLP 5.62).

Wittgenstein compares the relationship between I and the world with the relationship between the eye and the visual field. The eye is the viewpoint from which the visual field appears, and it is a necessary aspect of a visual field that it appears from a particular perspective. However, as Wittgenstein notes, 'really you do *not* see the eye. And nothing *in the visual field* allows you to infer that it is seen by an eye' (TLP 5.633). The visual field is always seen from somewhere, but the eye is not one of the facts presented within the visual field, and we do not learn anything about the eye by searching these facts – not even whether the eye is, in fact, an eye. In a similar way, the world is always approached from somewhere and experienced from a particular perspective – and never, for instance, from 'nowhere' – but this perspective is itself not part of the world, and we do not learn anything about the source of this perspective, what Wittgenstein calls the 'philosophical I' (TLP 5.641),[3] by searching through the facts of the world.

Wittgenstein uses the notion of the philosophical 'I' to show how the notion of 'the world' implies being experienced from a specific perspective. As Anscombe writes, the 'I' 'refers to the centre of life, or the point from which everything is seen' (1959: 168). Again, we do not learn anything new with the introduction of the Tractarian notions of world, logic, ethics and 'I', and no matter how much we investigate the actual world, there is, philosophically, nothing new to learn beyond what is already given for us with the fact that 'something *is*'. This is key to one of Wittgenstein's rather more difficult remarks about 'how much truth there is in solipsism' (TLP 5.62). The notion of the world is available only for an 'I' who can think and talk about the world, and this may seem to support the solipsistic point that the world depends on the 'I'. However, as the formal notion of the 'I' does not add anything to the world and simply leaves everything as it is, the truth in solipsism turns out to coincide with what the 'I' experiences, the world, and thus with realism, where, importantly, realism turns out to be just as uninformative as solipsism. As Wittgenstein writes, the 'I' in solipsism 'shrinks to a point without extension and there remains the reality co-ordinated with it' (TLP 5.64). Wittgenstein is making the conceptual point that the world has to be a world for someone, but he is not introducing a substantial notion of self, because as a purely formal feature of the world, the extensionless 'I' has no specific characterising features, and it is not anything in the world, 'not the human being,

---

[3] In this and following remarks, I have changed the translation of 'Ich' from 'self' to 'I' because I find it more loyal to the original German text.

not the human body, or the human soul, with which psychology deals' (TLP 5.641). The philosophically relevant 'I' is void of content and simply works as a tool of elucidation that shows us how the world is always tied to a specific perspective, which means that the 'I' cannot be expressed or described, but shows itself as 'the limit of the world – not a part of it' (TLP 5.641). Just as the world and language should be seen as reciprocal notions, we now come to see that the world and the philosophical 'I' are also reciprocal notions.

The philosophical 'I' has ethical relevance because it shows how any approach to the world is *specific*. It is part of the concept of an 'I' that it cannot attend to anything, everywhere, all at once; rather, it has to attend to something *in particular*. Furthermore, the 'I' cannot be a stationary perspective on the world because in a strictly formal sense, an 'I' is someone who has a life to lead, and its perspective on the world is shaped by the organisation established in this life. In this sense, 'world and life are one' (TLP 5.621). The form of organisation constituted by the 'I's approach to the world is thus both particular and active; an aspect of the formal notion of 'I' introduced in the remarks on ethics as a formal notion of *will*: 'It is impossible to speak about the will as the bearer of the ethical. And the will as a phenomenon is of interest only to psychology' (TLP 6.423). As the ethically relevant aspect of the philosophical 'I', the will, is formal, it is impossible to talk about and cannot alter any facts, not anything 'that can be expressed by means of language' (TLP 6.43).

This idea can be illuminated by looking at earlier remarks on the will in Wittgenstein's treatment of philosophical confusions about necessity and law (6.3n). Here, Wittgenstein considers whether the will has a necessary connection to the world, but he rejects this suggestion and underlines how anything in the world is independent of the will of the 'I'. Whether what we wish for happens or not is accidental, and if it does happen, this is indeed just 'a favour granted by fate, so to speak: for there is no *logical* connexion between the will and the world' (TLP 6.374). If someone were to object that they can in fact bring about changes in the world by acting on their will, Wittgenstein would reply that this objection misses the point. Even if there are, in some cases, causal connections between a person's willing and specific changes in the world, there is no *necessary* connection between what they will and what happens: even the best laid plans may turn out differently than they wanted them to. Any possible connection between the will and the world is *accidental*, and as such, these connections – as well as specific objects of will – are irrelevant to philosophy. What is philosophically relevant is that the will can only be moved by what the philosophical 'I' *can* come to will. The organisation of the world constituted by the will must thus be shaped by whatever the philosophical 'I' wills as relevant in life or, in other words, by what the 'I' finds to be of meaning and value.

This is the background against which it is possible to understand the mention of the will 'as bearer of the ethical' (TLP 6.423). Wittgenstein aims, in my view, to show that for the 'I' to come to will something is to come to see it as a valuable or meaningful object of will, something that is worth attending to, worth saying or doing (akin to Plato's point that we can desire only what we consider to be good, cf. Plato 1997). Wittgenstein is making the conceptual point that any approach to the world is shaped by active willing at the centre of the life of the 'I'. Moreover, relating to the world in terms of will makes some things stand out as important and central (and others not) in the 'I's' approach to the world, resulting in an organisation of the world that must, in turn, be understood in terms of value and meaning. This means, however, that whatever is made the object of will comes to be central not only to the life of the 'I', but also to the 'I's' organisation of the world. Life and world really 'are one' (TLP 5.621) because they are both organised by the same pattern of value established through the will of the 'I'. This also means that, as the bearer of ethics, the willing 'I' comes to take on responsibility for the way it organises the world in terms of value (see also Christensen 2018). In this way, the purely formal notion of the will of the philosophical 'I' introduces the possibility of ethics.

3.4 Is This Really Ethics? (TLP 6.422)

In the *Tractatus*, ethics arises because of the reciprocal notions of the world and the willing 'I', and it concerns how the will of the 'I' establishes an ethical perspective that organises the world in terms of meaning and value. As a way of relating to the world, this perspective is not reducible to psychological content; rather, it organises what the subject takes notice of, what facts it finds ethically relevant, and what it responds to and acts upon. The resulting organisation of the world shows in what the 'I' does and says, sees as valuable and what not, praises and condemns. This is why Wittgenstein of the *Tractatus* insists that there are no ethical sentences: ethics is not part of what we can describe and talk about but conditions how we approach and respond to what we can describe and talk about.

Ethics is indeed *transcendental* (TLP 6.421) because it is a condition of any possible engagement with the world. As such, ethics is a priori and empty of content, but it shows itself in what we say and think and in our dealings with the world, if we just refrain from trying to express it. Wittgenstein makes this point in a letter to his friend Paul Engelmann, remarking on a poem that 'this is how it is: if only you do not try to utter what is unutterable then *nothing* gets lost. But the unutterable will be – unutterably – *contained* in what has been uttered' (EN: 7). As some interpreters have noted, Wittgenstein saw indeed ethics as 'more properly located in the sphere of the poetic' (Jannik and Toulmin 1973: 193), but it is important to understand why this is; not because in poetry, we can 'kind of say' the ethical, but because poetry shows how ethics is already there, in the connection between 'I' and world, showing in everything we say, think, and do.

As already noted, this picture of ethics is quite different from the most influential views of ethics in moral philosophy, and this difference is in fact reflected in the *Tractatus*. One common assumption in moral philosophy is that ethics is normative and offers some form of action-guidance, but Wittgenstein dismisses this idea: 'When an ethical law of the form, "Thou shalt …", is laid down, one's first thought is, "And what if I do not do it?"' (TLP 6.422). According to Wittgenstein, there are no necessary ethical laws or guidelines, and even if we come to accept some such law, it is always, in principle, possible to challenge it (see also section 2.4 and Kremer 2001). The presentation of an ethical law does not in itself settle the question of whether to follow it. Wittgenstein also rejects another idea common in moral philosophy, that ethics aims at our individual moral improvement through an interpersonal system of praise and blame, for example by establishing forms of ethical punishment and reward. As he writes, 'ethics has nothing to do with punishment and reward in the usual sense of the terms. So our question about the *consequences* of an action must be unimportant. – At least those consequences should not be events' (TLP 6.422). At this point, Wittgenstein's rejection of the ethical relevance of consequences is no surprise: if ethics cannot influence anything in the world, its purpose cannot be to bring about particular facts, not even consequences traditionally considered to be morally good.

As Wittgenstein dismisses all attempts to connect ethics to anything external to ethics, any particularly ethical dimension of our actions must be internal; there 'must be some kind of ethical reward and ethical punishment, but they must reside in the action itself' (TLP 6.422). The idea is difficult, but Wittgenstein seems to say something like this: ethics is a pattern of value established in a person's dealings with the world, and as such, ethics is *completely dependent on* and *is at stake in* every single thing that person actually says and does. Ethics is not something *in* the world or life of the 'I', rather it is the 'I's' organisation of the world in terms of value and meaning that sets the framework or 'limit' for how this 'I' can meaningfully act and live. Ethics therefore does not change anything or add anything to the world; it only changes the totality or organisation of the world/life of the willing 'I'. As Wittgenstein notes: 'If the good or bad exercise of the will does alter the world, it can alter only the limits of the world, not the facts' (6.43). If someone feels compelled to object that the most important thing in ethics must be to attempt to change the world, this would be misguided because Wittgenstein neither supports nor contradicts this idea. Rather, he is showing what comes before any attempt to change the world (or anything else) because it conditions the possibility of talking about something as ethically important or valuable, namely the reciprocal notions of the willing 'I' and unity of world/life.

In bringing out these notions, Wittgenstein also shows that the unity of world/ life is simply what is given for the 'I'. This means that whatever the 'I' goes on to do, this will have to begin from an acceptance of whatever contingent version of world/life the 'I' is currently facing. 'The facts all contribute only to setting the task [*Aufgabe*], not to its solution' (TLP 6.4321; translation amended). Ethically, the willing 'I' has to accept world/life as it is, not because of some lack of power, but because the 'I' is placed in a world that does not bend to its will. This may come across as some form of ethical recommendation or advice for life on Wittgenstein's part: that we ought to stoically accept the facts as they are given to us, but this is not Wittgenstein's point. He is rather trying to counter the temptation to think that one can bring about change in the world simply by wishing it different. In my view there are completely everyday examples of this temptation: a person waiting in a line may come to find themself trying in some (magical) way to make their line move faster (or at least faster than the other lines) or, in a more serious situation, a person tending to a terminally ill spouse may find themself trying to change the world so that their beloved is not dying. We can all experience this urge to attempt to will the world to be different, but part of becoming a mature human being is to come to resist this temptation and accept that one cannot somehow simply 'will' the world to be different. This is what Wittgenstein is trying to clarify – that any engagement with the world will have to begin with an understanding and acceptance of the world as it confronts one. In Cora Diamond's words, that we look 'with clear eyes at the happenings of the world, at the happenings of the world being whatever they are' (2000: 154). Ethics is, in this sense, the task of finding out, without being distracted by philosophical confusions, what to do with one's world *as it actually is*.

Wittgenstein is trying to make us see that the 'task' to accept the world as it is, is not really a task at all because the attempt to will change is the result of confusions about our relationship with the world. Thus, we should resist the idea that there is anything in the *Tractatus* aimed at telling us how to live. Wittgenstein is rather trying to remove specific confusions that are diverting us from the activity of acting and living such as the fantasy that we can somehow will the world to be different than it actually is. Anything else is up to us, because the ethical perspective constituted by the will of the 'I' is a personal matter (as we see in the next chapter). In this sense, Wittgenstein of the *Tractatus* rejects that philosophical enquiry, such as that of the *Tractatus*, can settle any substantial ethical claims, and he opposes all forms of normative moral philosophy. In fact, by insisting that philosophy can only remove logical confusions, he also opposes all other forms of moral philosophy, even work on conceptual or existential issues, but in sections 4.2 and 5.1, I will argue that Wittgenstein later came to see this issue differently.

4 'A Lecture on Ethics' and Continuities in Wittgenstein's View of Ethics

4.1 'A Lecture on Ethics'

After publishing the *Tractatus*, Wittgenstein left academic philosophy to become a teacher. In this way, he stood by his general plea for silence and his remark to Hänsel that 'philosophy is silencing, the remainder is doing' (Engelmann 2021: 66). Still, as is well known, Wittgenstein in time came to question aspects of the Tractarian framework, and he somewhat reluctantly returned to philosophy. His only manuscript devoted exclusively to ethics, 'A Lecture on Ethics', was written and presented in 1929, shortly after his return to Cambridge and to serious engagement with philosophy (see Monk 1991: 276–8), and it is the last text that can be placed squarely within Wittgenstein's early view of ethics. The reason that I nonetheless discuss 'A Lecture on Ethics' in this transitional chapter is that Wittgenstein here discusses two issues that remain more or less stable throughout the intricate development of his thinking, the critique of theory in moral philosophy and the emphasis on the importance of the first-person standpoint in ethics.

The lecture was presented to a Cambridge society called 'The Heretics' on the 17th of November 1929, and it was written, not for philosophers, but rather for a general academic audience. Wittgenstein alludes to this in the beginning, when he says that as the lecture does not allow him enough time to explain a scientific matter such as logic, and as he does not want to present a popular science lecture, he will instead 'speak about something that I am keen to communicate to you' (LE: 37). I have already discussed how Wittgenstein in the lecture uses multiple synonyms to bring out an open-ended and inclusive view of ethics, and how he rejects philosophical enquires into ethics as nonsensical (see section 3.1). Here, I will focus on what Wittgenstein is 'keen to communicate', bringing out continuities between 'A Lecture on Ethics' and a Tractarian framework of elucidation, and how Wittgenstein in the lecture comes to struggle with this framework.

In the main part of the lecture, Wittgenstein elucidates his view of ethics in two quite different ways. First, he highlights a specific use of words as central to ethics and as characterised by a special form of necessity. Wittgenstein brings this out by contrasting two examples. In the first, he imagines playing tennis and being told by a bystander that he is playing rather poorly. To this Wittgenstein remarks that he can dismiss such a critique by saying that he has no wish to play tennis any better, and the bystander would then have to accept this as a perhaps regrettable but, in any case, acceptable reaction because it only makes sense to demand of someone that they improve their game of tennis if they have some interest in playing well. Wittgenstein then presents a second example, now involving a moral judgement: 'But suppose I had told one of you a preposterous lie and he came up to me and said "You're behaving like a beast" and then I were to say "I know I behave badly, but then I don't want to behave any better", could he then say "Ah, then that's alright"?' (LE: 39). This case is very different, as Wittgenstein notes: 'Certainly not; he would say "Well you *ought* to want to behave better"' (LE: 39). It is not possible to brush aside a reasonable moral judgement simply by insisting that one does not have any interest in behaving well or being good. In fact, Wittgenstein can only dismiss this judgement if he can show that it is *incorrect* – that even if his behaviour *seemed* beastly it really was not because the interlocutor was failing to take into account some relevant aspect of the situation; for example that Wittgenstein was lying only to protect another, vulnerable person involved.

Wittgenstein's point is that while some judgements are relative to specific interests and aims, others are not and ethical judgements are of this latter kind. He thus distinguishes between two types of uses of words, 'the trivial or relative sense on the one hand and the ethical or absolute sense on the other' (LE: 38), and he brings out how the 'ethical sense' implies necessity in the form of being non-dismissible. Wittgenstein here points to the familiar aspect of moral uses of words that we consider some forms of (reasonable) moral judgements – such as judgements that a person is being cruel, wicked or mean or doing what is cowardly, cheap, or disrespectful – to be always and immediately relevant for that person, independently of whether they actually care about these judgements, and independently of their specific inclinations, commitments, aims, and projects.

Wittgenstein illuminates this point by presenting a more peculiar example, contrasting the ordinary judgement that 'This is the right road to Granchester' with the judgement of '*the* absolute right road', which he describes as a road 'which *everybody*, on seeing it would, with logical necessity, have to go, or be ashamed for not going' (LE: 40). Wittgenstein calls the first judgement a judgement of *relative* value, because 'right' here is tied to some external and contingent aim, such as that of finding the fastest or prettiest road to Granchester, and he contrasts this with a judgement of *absolute* value, which would be relevant and binding for anyone, despite their aims or interest. The distinction between relative and absolute judgements is not a distinction between factual and evaluative judgements, because both types of judgements are indeed evaluative. Wittgenstein is rather illustrating that the ordinary way of giving meaning to evaluative judgements, by tying them to specific aims or wants, is not relevant in ethics (cf. Diamond 2011: 260). Wittgenstein later remarks: 'In ethics our expressions have a double meaning: a psychological one of which you can speak and a non-psychological one: "good tennis-player," "good"' (WVC: 92). We can meaningfully talk about relative evaluations and about any psychological facts that may happen to accompany ethical evaluations, but we cannot state the meaning of ethical expressions themselves.

Here, the continuity with the *Tractatus* becomes apparent. When Wittgenstein says that an absolute judgement would be one that everybody would 'with *logical* necessity, have to go' (LE: 40; italics added), this shows that he still models all forms of philosophically relevant necessity on logical necessity, seeing ethics, in some sense, as parallel to logic, as a formal condition of the world. The lecture thus helps clarify the difference between logic and ethics, as it ties moral necessity to action rather than to meaningful language, implying that ethics relates to actions that we necessarily have to do or be ashamed for not doing. Wittgenstein's picture of the parallel between ethics and logic thus seems to be something like this: if something is ethically right, we face an alternative: either we abide by it (and stop behaving like beasts, for example), or we necessarily fail in terms of acting and living, similar to how we, when we use language, face an alternative: either we engage in language uses that are logical, or we necessarily fail in terms of meaning and utter only nonsense. However, even if Wittgenstein is implying some form of moral necessity, this cannot be meaningfully expressed within his Tractarian framework.

In the lecture, Wittgenstein still holds the view that all facts are on the same level and that all meaningful language use concerns the description of facts, what he now terms '*natural* meaning' (LE: 40). Importantly, facts cannot be binding or have any 'coercive power' over us; there are no facts 'which everybody, independent of his tastes and inclinations, would necessarily bring about or feel guilty for not bringing about' (LE: 40, cf. Diamond 2000; Mulhall 2012: 26). As in the *Tractatus*, ethics is factless, and whatever form of necessity we find in Wittgenstein's examples, it does not concern facts and cannot find expression in language. Ethics, 'if it is anything, is supernatural' (LE: 40), in some way elevated beyond the world of facts. 'What is Good is Divine too. That, strangely enough, sums up my ethics' (CV: 5 [3]).

Wittgenstein's second major line of elucidation of ethics marks a departure from the Tractarian framework by introducing ethically relevant experiences, such as to '*wonder at the existence of the world*' and 'of feeling *absolutely* safe' (LE: 41). By presenting inner states as ethically relevant, Wittgenstein seems to move closer to the psychological side of the 'double meaning' of ethical uses of the words mentioned earlier, but he still insists that the introduced experiences cannot be captured in factual or psychological terms. If a person feels safe from specific dangers in specific situations, we can describe the facts that go into characterising this situation as 'safe', but no possible facts correspond to the experience of feeling absolutely safe because it is always possible that something unexpected could happen. For Wittgenstein, this means that 'it's nonsense to say that I am safe *whatever* happens' (LE: 42). Similarly, no specific facts correspond to the experience of wondering that the world exists because this wonder concerns the very fact of existence, 'that something *is*' (TLP 5.552). Again invoking a parallel between ethics and logic, Wittgenstein is 'tempted to say that what I am wondering at is a tautology, namely at the sky being blue or not blue. But then it's just nonsense to say that one is wondering at a tautology' (LE: 42). He also explores whether expressions of these experiences can have meaning as forms of *similes*, but for an expression to work as a simile, it must be 'about' something that we can also talk about independently of the metaphorical expression, and again, there are no facts of being absolutely safe or wondering at the world. Expressions of ethically relevant experiences cannot come to have meaning by comparison because there are no facts with which to compare them.

At this point in the lecture, Wittgenstein takes several rounds on what now appears to be a form of Tractarian merry-go-round: he investigates attempts to express the essence of ethics, explores whether these expressions correspond to a state of affairs, and when they turn out not to do so, he concludes that they are meaningless. In fact, the merry-go-round turns out to be inescapable, as Wittgenstein ultimately claims that if any expression introduced to indicate ethical value actually turned out to correspond to facts, he would then reject this expression as ethically irrelevant *on these very grounds*. As a case in point, when Wittgenstein reconsiders the experiences introduced earlier and notes that as these experiences are indeed facts, he 'must admit it is nonsense to say that they have absolute value' (LE: 43; cf. WVC: 93). These expressions of absolute value were nonsensical, Wittgenstein notes, not 'because I had not yet found the correct expressions, but ... their nonsensicality was their very essence' (LE: 44). Ethics and absolute value on the one hand and facts and meaning on the other are mutually exclusive, and the Tractarian merry-go-round set in motion by the attempt to meaningfully express absolute value will in fact go on forever because anything meaningful or factual is excluded from the very start.

Wittgenstein here echoes the Tractarian point that 'it is impossible for there to be propositions of ethics' (TLP 6.42). Still, the lecture is driven by aspirations radically different from those motivating the *Tractatus*. In the *Tractatus*, Wittgenstein has the purely therapeutic aims to show that ethics is not given with the facts, that acceptance of the facts conditions all ethical engagement with the world, and that all forms of philosophical enquiry into ethics must be rejected, making the *Tractatus* end with a recommendation of silence (cf. TLP 7). In 'A Lecture on Ethics', Wittgenstein still insists on rejecting philosophical engagement with ethics, but he now seems to have trouble reconciling that with his Tractarian framework. He continuously struggles against inclinations to 'indicate' points about ethics, for example, by 'characterising' it as 'necessary' and 'supernatural'. Furthermore, the descriptions of some of Wittgenstein's examples, such as calling someone a beast or wonder at the existence of the world, do not seem to be nonsensical (on any sensible understanding of nonsense), and this points beyond the *Tractatus* to forms of philosophical engagements with ethics that differ from those of wanting to express absolute value or the essence of ethics.

When Wittgenstein in the lecture speaks from a first-person standpoint with a motivation 'to communicate to you' (LE: 37), this seems to create tension with the purely therapeutic approach of the *Tractatus* and the insistence that ethics cannot be put into words. Wittgenstein is, of course, aware of this tension, and he addresses it at the end of the lecture, writing that 'the tendency of all men who ever tried to write or talk Ethics or Religion was to run against the boundaries of language. This running against the walls of our cage is perfectly, absolutely hopeless' (LE: 44). Still, Wittgenstein talks on and adds that this need to talk documents is 'a tendency in the human mind which I personally cannot help respecting deeply' (LE: 44). Wittgenstein is still dismissive of theoretical and philosophical approaches to ethics; here, silence remains the only right option because '[e]thics so far as it springs from the desire to say something about the ultimate meaning of life, the absolute good, the absolute valuable, can be no science. What it says does not add to our knowledge in any sense' (LE: 44; see also WVC: 68–9). The only way to put into place what philosophers are 'gassing' about in ethics is still 'by being silent about it' (EN: 143). The tension between the lecture and the *Tractatus* is thus to be explained with reference to the difference in Wittgenstein's standpoint; in the lecture, he is talking, not as a philosopher, but in the first person, presenting his own concern with ethics.

Nonetheless, I still think 'A Lecture on Ethics' is a paradigm case of a philosopher being held captive by a picture (cf. PI §115). Wittgenstein is moving within the framework of the general method of elucidation developed in the *Tractatus* that results in a picture of philosophy as caught in a mutually exclusive dichotomy between facts, meaning, knowledge, and science on the one hand, and world, I, value and ethics on the other (with logic balancing somewhat uncomfortably in the middle). In the lecture, this picture fuels the Tractarian merry-go-round that ultimately makes Wittgenstein unable to understand and describe completely ordinary phenomena, for example the role that moral judgements – such as 'You're behaving like a beast' – play in moral life. We can see Wittgenstein of the lecture as taking a step in the direction that would later lead him to acknowledge is that there are many other ways of engaging philosophically with ethics besides that of trying 'to say something about … the absolute good' (LE: 44). This insight is part of what makes Wittgenstein give up the dichotomous picture on which the source of ethics is unrelated to facts and somehow excluded from language, but before I investigate this change in his engagement with ethics, I will develop two points of continuity between his early and later writings on ethics.

4.2 The Critique of Ethical Theory

In 'A Lecture on Ethics', Wittgenstein is critical of the possibility of a science of ethics, and he emphasises the ethical importance of the first-person standpoint. In my view, both points survive the many changes in the later periods of Wittgenstein's writings, and they thus deserve a closer look. A good place to start is Wittgenstein's comments on these two points in conversations with the members of Vienna Circle, as recorded in notes by Friedrich Waismann.[4]

The conversations show that Wittgenstein's reservations towards philosophical engagements with ethics are directed primarily at attempts to develop ethical theories and explanations of ethics. In a conversation in December 1929, Wittgenstein says that it is '*a priori* certain that whatever definition of the good may be given … that does not and never will touch the essence of the matter' (WVC: 69). Much work in philosophy does not contribute to our understanding of ethics, Wittgenstein insists, and this makes it 'definitely important to put an end to all the claptrap about ethics – whether intuitive knowledge exists, whether values exist, whether the good is definable' (WVC: 68–9). Wittgenstein places himself in opposition to the mainstream in moral philosophy as the questions, he dismisses, were central to the form of the theory-driven moral philosophy practised in Wittgenstein's philosophical home in Cambridge, and they came to be at the heart of meta-ethics in the twentieth century. Wittgenstein later returns to this issue, admitting that science for example can record the way people make valuations and connect this to certain feelings and preferences, but he also immediately counters any attempt to use these psychological phenomena to

---

[4] The relevant conversations take place between 30 December 1929 and 17 December 1930, immediately after the presentation of 'A Lecture on Ethics'.

explain value. According to Wittgenstein, no feeling is in itself more valuable than any other, and 'the fact of being preferred has equally little claim to be something valuable in itself' (WVC: 116). Wittgenstein is not rejecting this or that explanation of values but rather the very possibility of providing scientific explanations of values: 'Is value a particular state of mind? Or a form attaching to some data or other of consciousness? I would reply that whatever I was told, I would reject, and that not because the explanation was false but because it was an *explanation*' (WVC: 116). Wittgenstein thus criticises scientific treatments of ethics because he thinks it impossible that scientific explanations could play any role in the attempt to substantiate or validate ethics.

In a similar way, Wittgenstein finds that theoretical approaches are simply irrelevant to ethics. 'If I were told anything that was a *theory*, I would say, No, no! That does not interest me. Even if this theory were true, it would not interest me – it would not be the exact thing I was looking for' (WVC: 116). A possible objection to this is that even if theories of ethics are not what we 'are looking for' in our engagement with ethics, this does not in itself discredit them. Wittgenstein is however making the stronger point that theories of ethics inevitably misconstrue or disfigure the phenomenon in question as they cannot grasp what is essential to ethics: 'If I could explain the essence of the ethical only by means of a theory, then what is ethical would be of no value whatsoever' (WVC: 117).

Wittgenstein also in other places opposes the idea of scientific discovery in ethics. In a remark from the same period, he considers the hypothetical case of someone (a philosopher, for example) who comes to think that he has somehow solved the problem of life and, with this solution, made life much easier. This man, Wittgenstein continues, 'need only tell himself, in order to see that he is wrong, that there was a time when this "solution" had not been discovered; but it must have been possible to live *then* too' (CV: 6 [4]). The 'solution' cannot be what makes it possible to live with meaning and value because this has always been possible, and this makes the discovery now appear 'like an accident' (CV: 6 [4]). Scientific problems call for discoveries that provide us with something *new*, new information or new theoretical explanations, but in Wittgenstein's view, ethical problems are different. Discoveries in ethics are discredited simply by the fact that we have managed to live and act well also before such discoveries were made, and whatever is required to engage with ethics therefore cannot be some form of discovery or specialised knowledge: 'What is ethical cannot be taught' (WVC: 117).

Wittgenstein's rejection of scientific and theoretical approaches to ethics is in line with his rejection of ambitions to develop theories and explanations in philosophy, in both the early and later thinking. As he remarks in a lecture: 'Are the same <u>sort</u> of reasons [as in Aesthetics] given elsewhere except in Ethics? Yes; in philosophy' (MWL: 352). In the later thinking, he also presents ethics as discontinuous with science, for example in a conversation in 1947 where he notes that for an artist, 'just the apparently trivial details of statement may seem as important as anything else, and perhaps the most important thing' and continues: 'So in ethics, too. Problems of morality are not like problems of engineering. ... A different sort of *Betrachtungprocess* (*process of investigation*)' (WPC: 39). Ethical problems are about importance and value, and this requires a perspective or way of looking where even the most trivial details can be important and crucial – in ethics, as well as in aesthetics and philosophy – but this importance, and here lies Wittgenstein's point, is not available from a scientific approach that emphasises precision, measurement, and causality (WPC: 38).

There is, however, an important change in Wittgenstein's view of the relationship between philosophy and ethics from the early to the later thinking. In the early thinking, there is really no room for lasting philosophical engagement with ethics because such engagements can only consist of confused attempts to develop scientific ethical theories (all the claptrap) or in clarification of the inexpressibility of ethics as a condition of our engagement with the world. It is difficult to say whether Wittgenstein holds on to the idea that we cannot express the essence of ethics because he does not discuss this question after 1930. What we know is that after 1930, Wittgenstein investigates moral discussions and ethically relevant uses of words in the very same way as he investigates all the other things we do in language, approaching moral language use as (at least potentially) meaningful and allowing for philosophical investigations of such uses (see section 5.2). Even if Wittgenstein, also in the later thinking, opposes ethical theories and discoveries in ethics, nothing indicates that he upholds his earlier resistance towards *all* philosophical investigations of ethics (contrary to Richter 1996, 2019).

4.3 Ethics Is Personal

In 'A Lecture on Ethics' we find another point of continuity between Wittgenstein's early and later thinking on ethics, as he connects ethics to a first-person standpoint. When Wittgenstein in the lecture departs from the Tractarian recommendation of silence in favour of an extensive and substantial engagement with ethics, he does so as a person who has something to communicate and who is speaking solely for himself. In the conversations with the Vienna circle, Wittgenstein remarks: 'At the end of my lecture on ethics I spoke in the first person: I think that this is something very essential. Here is nothing to be stated anymore; all I can do is to step forth as an individual and speak in the first person' (WVC: 117). In the *Tractatus*, ethics arises from the abstract 'I', but in the lecture Wittgenstein substantiates this by showing how ethics connects to the perspective of a *particular* person. The change of perspective from the impersonal, philosophical, and formal 'I' to the first person point of view of the lecture allows for an opening towards language in ethics, as Wittgenstein unfolds a specific ethical perspective and presents what is ethically important to him, such as respecting the tendency 'to say something about the ultimate meaning of life' (LE: 44).

Wittgenstein's emphasis on the first-person perspective is connected to his critique of explanations of ethics and theory-driven forms of moral philosophy. By drawing attention to his own standpoint, Wittgenstein is also criticising the idea that we can provide impersonal, rational foundations of specific ethical claims and thus ground them philosophically, exposing the philosophical illusion 'of wanting ethics to speak with an unquestioned, absolute authority' (Ong 2016: 220; see also Pianalto 2011). Considered from the perspective of philosophy, this may look as if Wittgenstein is revealing ethics to be ungrounded, but he is instead marking the place where we in ethics have to *leave* philosophy. As Engelmann notes: 'Without grounding, the choice of an ethical view amounts to adopting it, living it, in contrast to trying to justify it by means of logic, science, philosophy, or dogmatic religious views' (2021: 66). For Wittgenstein, ethical views or perspectives only come to have validity or grounding in the lives of individuals – this is his idea of the personal dimension of ethics (see also Christensen 2020a, pp. 111–28).

In 1931, Wittgenstein returns to the idea that we always speak from a personal standpoint in ethics: 'An ethical sentence [*Satz*] states "You shall do this!" or "That is good!" but not "These people say that this is good". But an ethical sentence is a personal act. Not a statement of fact. Like an exclamation of admiration' (PPO: 85, translation amended). Wittgenstein still rejects the view that ethical sentences record facts, including facts about what people call good, but in contrast to earlier, he now readily engages in philosophical investigations of personal statements of ethics. We may be tempted to interpret the characterisation of ethical sentences as 'exclamations of admiration' as a commitment to non-cognitivist, ethical expressivism in meta-ethics, but we should resist this temptation, because it conflicts with Wittgenstein's critique of ethical theories and does not help us make sense of the idea that an ethical sentence is a personal *act*. For Wittgenstein, ethical sentences are not only expressions of psychological states; they are also ways of *doing* something such as taking a stand on some ethical issue or making a commitment to a particular attitude, relationship, value, principle, or the like, which thereby becomes a part of what guides one's view of value in life and involvement with other people. In this view, ethics is established in what a person does, and what counts as ethical for them is what then shows in the ways they go on to talk, live, and act, for example in the ways they respond to others, what they aim for, and what they prize and condemn. This does not mean that we cannot find uniformity in ethics, or that a person's ethical convictions cannot be influenced by others or by what happens in their life (cf. CV: 95 [84]). Still, in principle, it is only possible fully to understand an ethical sentence by relating it to the person who says it, because its meaning depends on the ethical perspective of that person, who, therefore, also takes on ethical responsibility for what the sentence entails ethically.

By rejecting external justifications of ethical views, Wittgenstein rejects the possibility of answering the 'moral sceptic' (whoever this may be), because ethical justifications have to refer to something that has already made an ethical 'impression' on a person, that if, to their existing understanding of moral relevance. This means that is a person finds nothing of moral importance, it is not really possible to offer them moral justifications. The possibility of moral scepticism does not seem to bother Wittgenstein, though. Throughout his writings on ethics, he seems to take it as a stable feature of human life that we make certain ethical views or values central in our lives in this way – he treats ethics as part of our natural history, we might say (cf. PI 25). Wittgenstein instead investigates how moral justification works in our moral lives, and here, he notes, 'Nothing we do can be defended definitively. But only by reference to something else that is established' (CV: 23 [16]). Ethical justification takes place within the framework of ethical importance established in the life of an individual person, and as this framework is upheld by – or simply *is* – what this person considers ethically valuable, it cannot itself be justified.

The personal dimension of ethics also influences the way we engage in moral discussions with others, as reflected in a *Nachlass* remark: 'The ethical justification of an action must appeal to the man to whom I want to make it understandable' (TS 211: 207).[5] Wittgenstein's point is not that justification is more effective if it relies on something that the other person actually cares about but that a justification simply *fails as moral justification* if it does not rely on something that the other already values or can come to see as morally valuable because the fact that I myself see something as morally important is no guarantee that it carries the same weight – or any moral weight – in the life of another person. If I am truly concerned to justify something (a judgement or an action, for example) to another

---

[5] In references to Wittgenstein's *Nachlass*, I use the classification by Henrik-Georg von Wright (1969) and quote from the Bergen Electronic Edition (BEE). All translations from the *Nachlass* are my own.

person, I have to engage with moral concerns that the other person already takes to be (or can come to take to be) morally relevant, as Wittgenstein also notes: 'Just consider that the justification of an "ethical proposition" merely attempts to refer the proposition back to others that make an impression on you. If in the end you don't have disgust for this & admiration for that, then there is no justification worthy of that name' (PPO: 85). In this way, actual moral justifications show us something about the role of ethics in a person's life: 'What people accept as justification, –shows, how they think and live' (MS 130: 9). The personal character of ethics means that it may prove difficult to understand the ethical perspective of others, but these difficulties do not differ from the difficulties we may have in understanding the perspective of others generally, and if we strive to achieve at least a partial understanding of other people's moral commitments, we can from there engage in discussion about questions of ethical relevance.

Wittgenstein also touches upon the personal dimension of ethics in a discussion on ethics with Rush Rhees in 1945, returning to the idea that ethical sentences establish what a person considers to be of ethical importance in her life: 'Well, suppose I say Christian ethics is the right one. Then I am making a judgement of value. It amounts to *adopting* Christian ethics. It is not like saying that one of these physical theories must be the right one. The way in which some reality corresponds – or conflicts – with a physical theory has no counterpart here' (Rhees 1965: 24). Wittgenstein again notes that ethical views cannot, like scientific theories, be tested by some independent method, such as checking the facts, and that presenting something as the morally right view is a *doing* – it is to adopt this view as one's own. Wittgenstein also emphasises that ethical sentences are personal commitments to certain values or views in another remark from the same period: '*Denying* responsibility means, not *holding* anyone responsible' (CV: 73 [63]; see also Bouwsma 1986: 16). To say that there is no such thing as ethical responsibility is not to present a neutral, impersonal, or theoretical claim: it is to do something that shapes one's ethical perspective – in this case, that one does not relate to other people as subjects of responsibility, for example, because that one understands people's actions primarily as the result of outside determining forces such as genes or upbringing. Importantly, Wittgenstein's emphasis on the personal dimension of ethics does not imply that ethical sentences are essentially *private* (contra to Kelly 1995) or purely subjective. To use jargon from the lecture, Wittgenstein's point is that in presenting an ethical sentence, a person is doing something that has both an absolute and a personal dimension. On the one hand, they treat something as having absolute value and, on the other, they anchor this way of acting in their own way of living and talking. Ethics is both absolute and personal, a point to be revisited in the next chapter, where I focus on the remarks on ethics in Wittgenstein's later philosophy.

5 Wittgenstein's Later Writings on Ethics

5.1 Ethics in Wittgenstein's Later Writings

On 18 January 1929, economist John Maynard Keynes wrote in a letter to his wife that 'God has arrived. I met him on the 5.15 train' (Monk 1991: 255). Keynes was referring to Wittgenstein, who was returning to Cambridge surrounded by myths of genius and acclaim for the *Tractatus*. However, more or less from this day, Wittgenstein began to depart from this early work, as discussed already in the previous chapter. In this context, it is impossible to give an exhaustive presentation of the development from the *Tractatus* to the later thinking, so I will highlight only a few changes, central to the development in Wittgenstein's engagement with ethics.

In fact, Wittgenstein's overall view of philosophy changes only little. He still thinks that philosophical activity consists in the clarification of language, that philosophical considerations are not scientific, and that philosophers rather work by looking 'into the workings of our language, and that in such a way that these workings are recognized – *despite* an urge to misunderstand them' (PI §109). What changes in the later philosophy is first and foremost Wittgenstein's view of *language* and, with it, his view of what is needed in order to clarify language. In the *Tractatus*, Wittgenstein aims to develop a general method of elucidation, culminating in the general form of propositions (TLP 6), but in his later thinking, he gives up the idea that all of language shares the same logic and is available for the same form of elucidation. Instead, he develops a view of language as structured by a multitude of different grammars (cf. PI §90) established in our uses of words, but often lacking in perspicuity and thus calling for a variety of different forms of philosophical clarification (cf. §112).

In my view, a crude but ultimately correct way of describing this development is that in the *Tractatus*, Wittgenstein sees us as using language primarily to do one thing, to talk *about* something, but at the time of the *Philosophical Investigations*, he has come to see that we do all sorts of different things in language: we greet and count, name things, buy things (§1) and build things (§2), give orders and make measurements (§23), and so on, almost ad infinitum, because we live our whole lives in language. Wittgenstein introduces the term *language-game* to make visible how uses of language are part of our actions and activities, and how meaning arises in a 'whole, consisting of language and the activities into which it is woven' (§7), thus emphasising how philosophers must describe the many ways in which 'the *speaking* of language is part of an activity, or of a form of life' (§23). Language is entangled with specific ways of acting and living that are in turn shaped by the goals, purposes, and ideals of human beings. Language is thus, ultimately, embedded in and framed by our common form of life and the many forms of life we develop from this common form (cf. Boncompagni 2022).

In this way, what human beings find important, interesting, challenging, and ordinary is just as much part of what constitutes language as the need to talk about the world. As Avner Baz notes, Wittgenstein at this point considers 'the meaning of words as a function of the *use* that the words are put to, or may be put to – the *work* that the words perform, or are fit to perform – in *particular* circumstances, by *concrete* human beings' (2003: 482). An understanding of what a person says cannot be detached from an understanding of what that person is doing (or trying to do) and their reasons for saying what they do in this specific context. Wittgenstein thus also changes his conception of language-users, from the purely formal, philosophical 'I' of the *Tractatus* to a plurality of speakers with various background and projects, who are grieving, hurting, learning, and so on while communicating with and responding to each other.

By giving up the assumption of a unitary form of language, Wittgenstein also gives up the idea that there is one, single solution to 'the problems of philosophy' (TLP: 3) – which he now describes as a form of philosophical 'dogmatism' (PI §131) – and instead, he sees philosophy as engaged in continuous clarification of language. In philosophy, 'Problems are solved (difficulties eliminated), not a *single* problem', and because of this, there is 'not a philosophical method, though there are indeed methods, different therapies, as it were' (§133). Because language is diverse and dynamic, we often have difficulties understanding uses of language in specific cases, and philosophy addresses the problems that arise when 'we don't have *an overview* of the use of our words' (§122). The task of philosophy is to find relevant reminders (§127), to provide descriptions (§109), to present 'an object of comparison' (§130) or a 'surveyable representation' (§122) that may help us regain an overview of how we use language in specific cases (for introductions to Wittgenstein's later philosophy, see e.g. McGinn 1997; Stern 2004).

In general, there are both changes and continuities in Wittgenstein's view of ethics across the many developments from early to later thinking. I have already highlighted some continuities, but with the changes in his view of language, Wittgenstein's approach to ethics also changes. The dichotomous picture of ethics and facts disappears from the later remarks on ethics, and as noted earlier, his view of how philosophy can engage with ethics also changes. Wittgenstein now thinks that philosophy can investigate ethically relevant language uses beyond attempts 'to say something *about* . . . the absolute good' (LE: 44, italics added). One example is that Wittgenstein, for years, returns to an investigation of ethical uses of the word 'good'; another is that he now also emphasises the philosophical importance of attending to how ethics is embedded in specific circumstances that give rise to actual ethical problems. Wittgenstein holds on to the idea that philosophical engagement with ethics aims exclusively at clarification of language, but he eventually comes to think that this form of clarification can concern what is ethically specific and particular. As D. Z. Phillips sums up this view, 'What is general in ethics is conceptual elucidation and clarification. A philosopher may bring out the character of a specific moral perspective' (1992: 103). Wittgenstein's later approach to ethics thus differs remarkably from the purely formal elucidations of ethics in the *Tractatus*, as I will bring out in the following sections.

5.2 Uses of 'Good' and Ethically Relevant Uses of Language

When writing about the view of ethics in the later philosophy, an obvious place to start is the only place where the word 'ethics' appears in a manuscript that Wittgenstein himself completed for publication, in a remark in part I of the *Philosophical Investigations*. Interestingly, this remark has largely been ignored, despite the fact that Wittgenstein here introduces a way of investigating ethical concepts and thus goes some way to establish an approach to ethics in the later philosophy (see e.g. Stern 2012; Richter 2019). Wittgenstein mentions ethics in a section where he discusses the idea of family resemblance concepts, bringing out how concepts such as 'language' (§65) and 'game' (§66) cannot be defined with reference to one single feature shared by all the phenomena we call language or game. These concepts are rather held together by overlapping and criss-crossing similarities between phenomena, similar to 'the various resemblances between members of a family – build, features, colour of eyes, gait, temperament, and so on' (PI §67). The interlocutor of the *Investigations* objects that if we cannot clearly demarcate the application of a concept, it has no clear meaning, but Wittgenstein shows that even if we can only give a general and rough outline of a concept, if for example 'the concept of a game is a concept with blurred edges' (§71), this does not undermine its meaning because in many cases such rough demarcations are all we need, just as, in many cases, it makes perfect sense to say: 'Stay roughly there' (§71).

Wittgenstein brings out the important reminder that we draw up demarcations for specific purposes that call for more or less precise and determinate boundaries. Some cases may resist the attempt to work out clear demarcations altogether, as Wittgenstein points out by introducing an example where one would have 'to draw a sharp picture "corresponding" to a blurred one', adding:

> But if the colours in the original shade into another without a hint of any boundary, won't it become a hopeless task to draw a sharp picture corresponding to the blurred one? Won't you then have to say: 'Here I might just as

well draw a circle as a rectangle or a heart, for all the colours merge. Anything – and nothing – is right.' –And this is the position in which, for example, someone finds himself in aesthetics or ethics, when he looks for definitions that correspond to our concepts. (§77)

Wittgenstein clearly suggests that we should approach ethical – and aesthetical – concepts as family resemblance concepts, and not try to define them based on some shared, essential property or feature. As Wittgenstein writes in a manuscript in 1934, 'the use of the word "good" (in the ethical sense) is composed of a very large number of related games. Facets of use, so to speak. But it is precisely the connection between these facets, their kinship, that creates a concept here' (MS 140: 33). Philosophers need to attend to how ethical concepts hold together a family of different meanings that may 'shade into' each other without us being able to draw a clear line around their individual meanings.

This is not all that Wittgenstein says about ethical concepts in this context. In response to the objection against family resemblance concepts that it would be almost impossible to get an overview of the many meanings of such a concept, Wittgenstein says: 'always ask yourself: How did we *learn* the meaning of this word ("good" for instance)? From what sort of examples? In what language-games? Then it will be easier for you to see that the word must have a family of meanings' (§77). We learn a word like 'good' in diverse circumstances and they all contribute to its meaning. As Wittgenstein notes, 'A child generally applies a word like "good" first to food' (LC: 2), and more ethical uses are learnt as part of evaluations of ways of playing and hanging out with other children, as part of admonitions or encouragements, prohibitions or ideals offered by authorities such as parents or teachers, and in early discussions about what is involved in becoming a (remotely) good person. Moreover, even if we try to limit investigations to recognisable ethical uses of good, we find great variety of uses, as we use the word 'good' to talk about actions, outcomes, and people, to praise, recommend, prescribe, or evaluate, and we, even in ethical contexts, use 'good' to talk about instrumental as well as intrinsic value. This variety challenges the idea, running through much of moral philosophy, that there is one, distinct feature in play in all these ways of using 'good', and §77 is important because Wittgenstein here provides us with an alternative in the form of 'two clear-cut proposals about ethical concepts ...: they cannot be defined, for they have a family of meanings [. . . and] we should look at how we learn the meaning of such terms in order to appreciate this' (Stern 2012: 59).

Another source of insight into Wittgenstein's investigations of ethical concepts are several sets of notes written by students and colleagues from his lectures in the 1930s. In these lectures, Wittgenstein again shows how ethical concepts like 'good' cannot be defined (AWL: 96, MWL: 324–5) and recommends connecting investigations of their meaning to the learning of ethically relevant uses of words (MWL: 325). Wittgenstein also suggests other ways of investigating 'good' such as looking at the way its meaning is shaped by what comes to be established as the shared meaning in actual discussion of goodness. 'Each <u>way</u> in which A can convince B that x is <u>good</u>, fixes a meaning in which "good" is used – fixes the grammar of the discussion' (MWL: 325). Wittgenstein is not implying that the meaning of good is completely up to A and B; rather, that language users in specific discussions for specific purposes settle on the grammar in play in their discussion and thus on a meaning (or meanings) of 'good'. In the investigation of the meaning of 'good', we have to distinguish between the diverse families that make up this meaning, and one way to do so is thus to investigate how the word plays different roles in discussions of different topics, for example how the meaning of 'good' changes in discussions of actions or outcomes or people, because '[t]he way in which you use "good" in particular case is <u>partly</u> defined by the topic you're talking about' (MWL: 325).

In one lecture, Wittgenstein criticises the search for a unified definition of 'good', dominant in the moral philosophy of his time, as an unproductive approach to ethical concepts: 'One way of looking at Ethics is to say meaning of "good" must be what is common to all things we call "good" . . .: I said this was far too simple' (MWL: 332).[6] The preoccupation with definitions and the hunt for a common feature of the 'good' is problematical because it blinds philosophers to the variety of uses of good, but also, and here Wittgenstein adds a new point, because it blinds them to the possibility that this common feature may not be what we need to understand the meaning of 'good' or its role in ethics. 'We can't find out meaning of "good", by looking for what <u>all</u> cases have in common: even if there <u>is</u> something in common, we <u>may</u> never use "good" for that' (MWL: 324). When we are uncertain about how to understand 'good' or whether something is in fact ethically good, these difficulties may not be helped by pointing to some shared feature in everything we call good because this feature may not be relevant for an understanding of good in the context in question. In a conversation with O. K. Bouwsma, Wittgenstein raises a related worry about the philosophical preoccupation with definitions. Even if it is possible to offer a definition of 'good', this definition may not be relevant to actual struggles in understanding ethical goodness. Discussing a case about a person in doubt about the good, Wittgenstein asks: 'Would someone is such a case

---

[6] When 'Ethics' is capitalised in the lecture notes, and often also in Wittgenstein's own writings, the word refers to the philosophical discipline of moral philosophy.

ask for a definition? If he asked for a definition, to what end would he do this? Guidance? How could it guide him?' (Bouwsma 1986: 40). According to Bouwsma, Wittgenstein brooded over this question, but finally said that a definition could be relevant for the person in doubt, but 'in order for it to serve him, it would have to do so as a resolution by which he would come to alter attitudes' (1986: 40). Even if a definition could be ethically relevant by influencing the attitudes of a person (and I turn to Wittgenstein's notion of ethical attitudes in the next section), this definition is only a small part of the language-game that surrounds the word 'good', and other, more important parts, Wittgenstein goes on to say, are made up of concepts such as 'ought', 'shame', 'conscious' and 'evil', and so on (1986: 41).

In the lectures, as in §77 of the *Investigations*, Wittgenstein compares ethical and aesthetical ways of talking and brings out how philosophical approaches are shaped by some rather narrow and sometimes distorting assumptions. In a discussion of how we choose between alternatives and justify such choices in ethics and aesthetics, Wittgenstein notes: 'Many people have said: One always does what gives most pleasure', adding: 'Something queer happens here' (MWL: 336). The assumption that we choose based on comparison and maximisation of pleasure is central in classic, British utilitarianism, and it also dominated mid-twentieth century British moral philosophy. However, as Wittgenstein points out, we can easily find cases where ethical action does not involve overt, individual choice or reference to the maximisation of pleasure (or anything else):

> Sometimes you do choose an alternative because more pleasant; but very often you don't.
>
> So when I jump into water to rescue someone, though very afraid of getting drowned, I don't weigh any alternatives at all. . . .
>
> What 'choice' does happen, if there is one, when you jump in to save someone? Not a choice between pleasures, nor yet between pains. There will be pros & cons, & then something will happen. But there is nothing which I compare, in the sense in which I compare 2 pieces of chalk to find which is longest. (MWL: 337)

If a person jumps into the water to save another person from drowning, it is not always clear that they actively choose to do so in any straightforward sense of choice. Even if it makes sense to talk of choice here – and this is Wittgenstein's main point – this choice does not take the form of a process of weighing two alternatives in terms of pleasure, and the decision does not depend on a judgement of which alternative would be most pleasant, in relation to neither the person's own pleasure nor some more general perspective. Just as likely, the person will not have cause for thought, as they already know what to do (if they think anything at all, it may just be: I need to save that person), and we get a wrong understanding of what moved them to jump in the water, if we construed this in terms of a process of comparing or weighing alternatives.

Wittgenstein thus challenges the assumption that hedonism and maximisation play a general role in ethical judgement. To this he adds that philosophers have ascribed them this role only because of their preoccupation with the word 'good', which has allowed parts of the grammar of comparative uses of 'good' to seep into philosophical investigations, blinding philosophers to the fact that ethics, like aesthetics, is not (at least not primarily) a comparative activity: 'All ethics seems to be based on this illusion. It is said that this human being is better than that and immediately one believes that one is dealing with a series of quantitative determinations like a series of weights' (TS 219: 11). In aesthetics and ethics, we are of course interested in what is beautiful and good, but this does not necessarily entail, as philosophers sometimes assume, that we are even more interested in what is more or most beautiful and best. As Wittgenstein notes: 'You use beautiful in: "Look how marvellous". But you don't say "This isn't beautiful enough". & so you don't in Ethics "This action isn't good enough"' (MWL: 340).

Wittgenstein reproaches moral philosophers for lacking attention to the variety in ordinary language use, also in relation to ethics: 'If I had to say what is the main mistake made by philosophers of the present generation, including Moore, I would say that it is that when language is looked at, what is looked at is a form of words and not the use made of the form of words' (LC: 2). According to Wittgenstein, moral philosophers should shift their attention away from the investigation of specifically ethical concepts towards explorations of how we talk about ethical problems including the many different ways that we talk about ethical problems without invoking any specialised ethical vocabulary. By suggesting that the question of whether a sentence belongs to ethics is to be settled, not by identifying specific 'form of words', but rather by looking at the way we use words, Wittgenstein not only resists the attempt to give definite definitions to ethical concepts but also refuses to delineate ethics by restricting it to a specific vocabulary. He thus challenges the idea that moral philosophy's 'subject matter' can be specified and delineated with reference to specifically moral concepts.

In one of the most influential articles on Wittgenstein's later ethics, Cora Diamond develops this point by considering the suggestion that 'a sentence's belonging to ethics is a classification by use rather than by subject matter' (1996: 237). Diamond argues that a sentence has an ethical use if it allows us to do something that we want or need to do in moral life in different ways, for example if it allows us to see something as morally relevant, shapes our moral attention, or helps us understand how to act in particular situations. As Diamond sums up:

> Whole sentences, stories, images, the idea we have of a person, words, rules: anything made of the resources of ordinary language may be brought into such a relation to our lives and actions and understanding of the world that we might speak of the thinking involved in that connection as 'moral'. There is no limit to be set. (1996, 248; cf. Mulhall 2012)

On this reading, Wittgenstein rejects the possibility of identifying ethical relevance prior to investigations of ethically relevant forms of language-use. This rejection is in line with the view of ethics, running through all of his thinking, as a way of organising one's life in terms of meaning and value because on this view, ethics is not an area of life or the world that can be delimited independently of whatever actually takes on value in our lives. Wittgenstein thus uses the comparison between ethical and aesthetic uses of language to call for a new way of investigating ethics in philosophy that goes beyond investigations of specific types of words and sentences: 'We are concentrating, not on the words "good" or "beautiful" … but on the occasions on which they are said – on the enormously complicated situation', Wittgenstein says in one lecture and continues, 'How far this takes us from normal aesthetics [and ethics – T]. We don't start from certain words, but from certain occasions or activities' (LC: 2–3). In moral philosophy, we should not just look at isolated, abstract unities such as concepts and choices but also at the ways that concepts and choices and other forms of moral concerns are embedded and unfold in concrete situations in the lives of actual human beings. As Lars Hertzberg presents Wittgenstein's point: 'We should look at the context: the nature of the moral concern expressed is not determined by the use of certain words. Everything depends on what the speaker is doing in uttering those words in a context' (2002: 256). In fact, Wittgenstein himself engages in such contextual investigations of examples, and to these we now turn.

5.3 Context, Particularity, and Objectivity

A central source for an understanding of the later view of ethics is a set of notes that Wittgenstein's friend Rush Rhees made of their ongoing conversations (Rhees 1965 and 2001: 410–11; WPC: 26–30). In one such conversation, Wittgenstein remarks that 'it was strange that you could find books on ethics in which there was no mention of a genuine ethical or moral problem' (1965: 21), thus recommending one way in which philosophical investigations of ethics could proceed, namely by looking at people's actual ethical problems. In the conversation, Rhees suggests that they consider the example of a man who considers himself faced with the choice of either leaving his wife or abandoning his work within cancer research. Wittgenstein notes that the man may adopt one of a number of possible attitudes towards these two options that each highlight different aspects of the situation as the most important or valuable, the man's obligations to his wife or the importance of his research. The man may also connect the options to his past actions and choices in different ways, just as other people may have very different attitudes towards the situation: 'Suppose I am his friend, and I say to him "Look, you've taken this girl out of her home, and now, by God, you must stick to her." This would be taking up an ethical attitude' (1965: 22). To Wittgenstein, an ethical attitude seems to involve a comprehensive, ethical perspective on the situation within which one of the options comes to stand out as the right one that ought to be chosen, while others fade in importance. If Wittgenstein, as a friend, had instead observed that 'your wife is a capable woman and would not want to stand in way of your research', the ethical attitude reflected in his remark would have led to different moral recommendations.

Wittgenstein also remarks that if the man has already adopted some well-established and comprehensive ethical system such as certain types of Christian ethics, this would settle the question, as he would then have to stay with his wife – presumably because Christian ethics, in Wittgenstein's understanding, cannot recommend leaving one's spouse. Through reflection on his predicament, the ethical attitude of the man may come to change, just as it may be influenced by what he chooses to do – ethics is in this way not only personal but also contextual and dynamic. 'He may say, "Well, thank God I left her: it was better all around." Or maybe, "Thank God I stuck to her." Or he may not be able to say "thank God" at all, but just the opposite,' Wittgenstein remarks and concludes: 'I want to say that this is the solution of an ethical problem' (Rhees 1965: 23). The ethical problem arises when the man cannot settle on an ethical attitude that provides him with a reason for one of his options as the right option, and the problem remains until he establishes a coherent attitude of the value of his choices and actions, past and future – even if this attitude may point to some of his choices as wrong (if he is not able to say 'thank God' at all). The choice of one option may not in itself be enough to solve his *ethical* problem as this problem rather arises because of a tension in his own ethical attitude towards the situation, for example the value he places on his marriage and his research respectively.

Wittgenstein clearly thinks that there are many possible ethical attitudes as well as more comprehensive ethical systems, and he also explicitly cautions against the failure to acknowledge ethical variety in philosophy. In considering different systems of ethics there may be 'a temptation to interpret what adherents of a different ethics are doing and saying in terms of some conception of good that we ourselves hold, and to say that this interpretation is what they really mean' (WPC: 28). In investigations of ethical questions, we should not assume that we already know what is ethically relevant, and we should take seriously what people actually present as ethical reasons, even if these reasons may be very different from anything we would ourselves consider ethical or important. We should thus refrain from 'assuming that reasons must really be of a different sort from what they are seen to be' (Rhees 1965: 26).

In the conversations with Rhees, Wittgenstein elaborates on this inclusive view of what can be brought to have ethical relevance. When Rhees mentions a slogan by Herman Göring, '*Recht ist das, was uns gefällt*' ('Right is what pleases us'), Wittgenstein remarks that 'even that is a kind of ethics. It is helpful in silencing objections to a certain attitude' (1965: 25). This ready acceptance of what many would see not as an ethical attitude but rather as a demonstration of power – and an unethical one at that – may seem to imply acceptance of a form of radical ethical relativism, challenging the objective character of ethics. Wittgenstein does however reject this and argues that the existence of actual ethical disagreement and various systems of ethics does not by itself amount to a theoretical insight into the truth of relativism. Furthermore, when discussing what could justify an action, Wittgenstein remarks that this variety of systems of ethics does not undermine the individual systems because one's awareness that others have different ethical attitudes to an ethical question does not mean that one must 'cease to adhere to one system of ethics – and in this sense be indifferent – and if I do adhere then ... I will recognise reasons which are decisive [for or against the action]' (WPC: 28).

In a similar vein, Wittgenstein thinks it misguided when philosophers, moved by fear of relativism, try to develop ethical theories to justify the *right* ethical systems because, as ethics requires personal commitment, it can never be the task of philosophy to evaluate the ethical validity of particular ethical attitudes. One time, when Rhees mentions the opposition between Christian morality and Nietzsche's critique of Christianity, Wittgenstein remarks that if Rhees wants to try to solve such a conflict between ethical systems, 'go ahead and good luck to you. It is nothing I could do or dream of doing' (WPC: 52). In a philosophical discussion, there is no way to decide between ethical systems because here, we do not know what the criteria could be. Of course, the evaluation of ethical systems is not complete arbitrary; there 'is argument, and in the course of the argument there are reasons for and against', but 'there isn't generally proof' (WPC: 28), as Wittgenstein observes, because the weight of arguments hinges on the place and importance of these arguments in people's lives, not on their theoretical merits. We cannot provide general and impersonal proof of a particular ethical system because we can only establish ethical importance by adopting an attitude as the right one, and this move is very different from making a theoretical argument – in fact, it is not a move in philosophy, but a different form of activity, that of engaging in moral life.

In the later philosophy, Wittgenstein thus still rejects the idea, central in much normative moral philosophy, that philosophy can develop justified normative guides for right conduct (see e.g. Diamond 1996; Wisnewski 2007). For Wittgenstein, the role of philosophy is not to decide which ethical system we ought to adopt, or specify what kind of people we ought to be, but to clarify the very possibility of an ethical attitude, showing how we relate to our world and lives in ways that establish crucial differences between what we find good and bad, valuable and neutral, right and wrong. In fact, Wittgenstein is trying to make philosophers give up the idea that the objectivity of ethics depends on the possibility of providing theoretical proof of some specific ethical system, and instead turn their attention to investigations of the roles that objectivity plays in ethical thinking and discussions, for example describing how adopting an ethical system in itself involves a claim to objectivity: 'If you say there are various systems of ethics you are not saying that they are all equally right. That means nothing. Just that it would have no meaning to say that each man was right from his own standpoint. That could only mean that each judges as he does' (Rhees 1965: 24).

For Wittgenstein, the idea that ethical relevance is dependent on personal ethical commitments does not challenge the idea of objectivity, because it is not up to philosophy to secure or validate this objectivity. As Benjamin De Mesel notes, it is 'true that Wittgenstein, both early and late, saw ethics as deeply personal and bound up with people's deepest concerns and commitments. It does not follow, though, that he saw ethics as essentially subjective. That only follows if what is deeply personal and bound up with people's deepest concerns and commitments cannot be objective' (2017: 13; see also section 4.3).

5.4 Ethics and the 'Problem of Life'

In Wittgenstein's engagement with ethics in his later thinking, two themes stand out as central, the confrontation with the problem of life and the relationship to the other, and I will consider these themes in this and the next section. Already in the early thinking, we saw how Wittgenstein connects ethics to of the most debated questions in philosophy, namely that of the meaning or problem of life, and in a remark from the later period, he notes that the problem of life arises when we cannot find a way to live that we find bearable, personally as well as morally: 'I may well reject the Christian solution of the problem of life (salvation, resurrection, judgement, heaven, hell) but this does not solve the problem of my life, for I am not good & not happy' (PPO: 169). The problem of life relates both to ethical considerations (of how to be 'good') and to considerations of prosperity and fulfilment in a wider sense (of how to be 'happy'), and the fact that Wittgenstein thinks this problem could be given a Christian solution shows that he sees an intimate connection between ethics and religion, as they both are relevant to the question of how to live one's life (see e.g. Schönbaumsfeld 2023).

In later writings, Wittgenstein more specifically connects the problem of finding life meaningful and bearable with the ethical problems of establishing value and importance by means of the notion of a person's attitude (*Verhaltens*) to life: 'If life becomes hard to bear we think of improvements ("a change of situation"). But the most important & effective improvement ("change"), in our own attitude, hardly occurs to us, & we can decide on this only with the utmost difficulty' (CV: 60 [53]). As we saw, in his discussions with Rhees, Wittgenstein uses the word 'attitude' for the way we organise the world in terms of ethical importance and value, and in this remark, he brings out how problems of life do not arise from the circumstances of one's life considered in isolation, but from the way one approaches these circumstances, that is, how one understands them as presenting possibilities, necessities, demands, and so on. This point is related to the Tractarian idea of the ethical perspective of the 'I' on the world, but Wittgenstein now presents the ethical attitude as a result of active engagement in life and as something that we can reflect on and change, thereby changing the way we approach our lives and the problems we face here.

When Wittgenstein says that the most important improvement is to change one's attitude, thus making the attempt to change the situation ethically secondary, this should not be interpreted as a recommendation of passivity. He is rather offering a reminder that what is *ethically* relevant is the tension between the way one approaches a situation – what one sees as important and how one thinks one should act and respond – and what is actually at play in the situation, and because of this, the ethically relevant change is a change in the way one relates to the situation or the people involved, for example by moving from acceptance to rejection or from being a bystander to active engagement. To flesh out Wittgenstein's point, if a situation presents me with an ethical challenge, something I find unacceptable, unjust, or cruel, this only becomes an ethical *problem* if I, despite my view of the situation, do nothing to change it. That is, it raises an ethical problem for me if I for example notice injustice without responding to it, but it does not raise an ethical problem if I notice injustice and fight it – even though it may, of course, raise all sorts of other problems – because this kind of coherence in attitude and engagement in life is what is required for living ethically.

Wittgenstein also reflects on the problem of life in several remarks written in 1937. He notices that he has a vague, disruptive feeling concerning 'the problem of this my life' (MS 118: ii), and this initiates a trail of reflections, culminating in a remark now published in *Culture and Value*: 'The solution of the problem you see in life is a way of living which makes what is problematic disappear. The fact that life is problematic means that your life does not fit life's shape. So you must change your life, & once it fits the shape, what is problematic will disappear' (CV: 31 [27]). The problem of life arises because Wittgenstein lives in a way that does not 'fit life's shape', and the solution he is looking for does not come in the form of a general theory of how to live, but in the form of a way of living that will dissolve the tension between his way of living and 'life's shape'. To recall a point made in connection to his early thinking, Wittgenstein is not calling for an uncritical acceptance of 'life's shape' – the circumstances of his life – rather, he is drawing attention to the fact that, at any particular point in life, one is placed in a life and a context that is, in an important sense, already *there*. One always finds oneself at a certain place and time, with certain abilities and weaknesses, one stands in certain relationships and has certain possibilities and challenges, and so on. In this sense, the shape of one's life is already given, and in drawing attention to this, Wittgenstein is cautioning us that we should refrain from wishful thinking about the possibility simply to live life from somewhere *else*. He is warning us against moral escapism, we might say. As Wittgenstein writes in another context: 'To be in the world – that is what counts . . . to be in it, as it is. That is: not to make up a novel and then be astonished and outraged by the lack of correspondence between it and the world' (MS 120: 8 r).

In the previous remark, Wittgenstein also suggests that engagement with the problem of life and the search for the right way of living is both an important and a continuous undertaking, and he asks whether anyone who does not realise this 'is blind to something important, indeed to what is most important of all? Wouldn't I like to say that he is living aimlessly – just blindly like a mole as it were; & if he could only see ("look up"), he would see the problem?' (CV: 31 [27]). A person who does not see a problem in life is blinded, not just to specific problems, but to the most important part of living, namely the task of reflecting on this life. Wittgenstein's remark thus resonates with the Socratic point that the unexamined life is not worth living: 'Or shouldn't I say: someone who lives rightly does not experience the problem as *sorrow*, hence not after all as a problem, but rather as a joy, that is so to speak as a bright halo round his life, not a murky background' (CV: 31 [27]). Wittgenstein is suggesting that it should be an integrated and welcome part of life to continuously address the problem of one's life, but without being worried by it, that engaging with the question of how to live is itself a part of the attempt to live ethically.

Together with his notion of an active and changeable ethical attitude towards life, Wittgenstein thus introduces a demand for continuous reflection on this attitude and our approach to the circumstances of our lives.

Wittgenstein not only introduces a demand to address and reflect on the problem of life but also suggests that honest and genuine reflection on oneself and one's life will actually lead to an attempt to live better, writing: '*Nobody can say with truth of himself that he is filth*. For if I do say it, though it can be true in a sense, still I cannot myself be penetrated by this truth: otherwise I should have to go mad, or change myself' (CV: 37 [32]). In one sense, Wittgenstein is making the grammatical point that if a person calls themselves 'filth' and remains unaffected, they really do not mean what they say, but he also takes this point to have practical implications by suggesting that a person's honest and serious acknowledgement of their shortcomings must lead to an effort to do better – or they will need some kind of excuse to deflect the practical consequences of their self-assessment. Honest self-assessment will in this way lead to self-improvement. Wittgenstein continuously returns to this connection between self-assessment and self-improvement in reflections on his own ethical aspirations: 'Let me hold on to this that I do not want to deceive myself. That is, a certain demand which I acknowledge as such I want to admit to myself again and again as a demand', Wittgenstein writes and continues: 'From that it follows that I will either meet the demand or suffer from not meeting it, for I cannot prescribe it to myself & not suffer from not living up to it' (PPO: 175). In Wittgenstein's s view, if a person seriously acknowledges some ethical demand, it becomes central to that person's understanding of the right way of living, and they are then also forced to consider their own ethical standing in relation to this demand as well as their other ethical commitments.

According to Wittgenstein, it is in fact always possible to question one's own motives or to suspect oneself of not trying hard or seriously enough, ethically, and he continuously struggles with this challenge, suspecting that what seem to himself and others to be admirable motives really are the expression of something more base: 'It is hard to understand yourself properly since something you *might* be doing out of generosity & goodness is the same as you may be doing out of cowardice and indifference. To be sure, one may act in such & such a way from true love, but also from deceitfulness & from a cold heart too' (CV: 54 [48]). Any understanding of one's own ethical standing is characterised by inherent insecurity, especially because one always faces a strong temptation to make oneself look better than one is, to others as well as to oneself. This temptation to avoid confrontation with one's possible moral failings often stands in the way of honest self-assessment. 'Know thyself & you will see that you are in every way again and again a poor sinner', Wittgenstein writes and admits: 'But I don't want to be a poor sinner & seek in all manner to slip away' (PPO: 111). Wittgenstein here touches upon a topic rarely treated in moral philosophy, that we generally find it extremely difficult to acknowledge that we are somehow morally in the wrong, and he also investigates some of the many strategies that we use to avoid facing our moral flaws such as turning a judgemental eye towards the weaknesses or transgressions of other people or invoking irrelevant justifications to excuse our moral wrongdoings or sins of omission. 'If someone prophesies that the generation to come will take up these problems & solve them that is usually a sort of wishful thinking, a way of excusing oneself for what one should have accomplished & hasn't' (CV: 29 [25]). In many cases, where we insist that the resolution of an ethical problem will have to wait to be taken up later, we are really attempting to relieve ourselves of the nagging suspicion that we are currently failing to act – this is, for example, a possible (and I think likely) interpretation of some of our reactions to the problems involved in countering climate change.

Throughout his life, Wittgenstein returns to the word 'decency', as when he, after finishing the manuscript for the *Tractatus*, remarks to Hänsel that 'the remainder is doing, [which] means: becoming a decent person' (Engelmann 2021: 66). For Wittgenstein, decency ties together an ethical aspiration for self-betterment and honest self-assessment because, as he writes, anyone 'who is half-way decent will think himself utterly imperfect' (CV: 51 [45]). To strive to be a morally decent person is to acknowledge that one is less than morally perfect and that there is still room for improvement in a way that moves one's attention away from the assessment or judgement of others and returns it to engagement with one's own moral standing. The idea of decency thus sums up Wittgenstein's idea that ethics involves a requirement to work towards a clear understanding of oneself and one's place in the world and to live in a way that reduces the difference between one's way of living and one's ethical ideals. This view of ethics is formal rather than substantial or determinate as it does not provide any positive guidelines or requirements about what to do or how to live. Thus, we cannot, for example in philosophy, etablish a general and substantial 'content' in ethics. 'Look after making yourself more decent' (CV: 35 [30]). And: 'You must strive' (MS 120: 17 v), as Wittgenstein sums up his view. According to Wittgenstein, ethics is the continuous struggle to keep trying to do better, and to see this struggle not as a 'sorrow' but as 'a bright halo round' one's life (cf. CV: 31 [27]). Still, Wittgenstein does not ignore the difficulties involved in striving ethically. As he notes in a diary entry, drawing on the idea of the absolute, central in his early ethical writings, 'the only absolute is, to battle through life towards death, like a fighting, a charging soldier. Everything else is wavering, cowardice, sloth, thus wretchedness' (PPO: 197).

5.5 The Other in Wittgenstein's Later Writings

In contrast to the thoroughly individualised perspective of the early writings on ethics, the relation to the other plays a central role in many of Wittgenstein's later remarks on ethics, even if this aspect of his later thought has so far received relatively little attention. In fact, the very activity of doing philosophy is relational or dialogical in Wittgenstein's later writings. In the *Philosophical Investigations*, the exploration of a philosophical problem is a communal activity, where several voices strive to understand different approaches to and perspectives on the problem at hand in a shared search for clarity. As David Stern puts it, the '*Investigations* is best understood as inviting the reader to engage in a philosophical dialogue', and the 'result is best understood, I believe, as emerging out of the reader's involvement in the dialogue' (2006: 220; see also Christensen 2020b). Wittgenstein's later work is in this sense interpersonal and takes the form of exchanges between the philosopher, the interlocutor, and the reader.

This notable development away from the strict individualism of the early writings is also reflected at the opening of the *Investigations*, as Wittgenstein makes a striking contrast between an individualistic and a relational approach to language. In §1, we are presented with the child Augustine, who approaches language from an inner and purely individual perspective, as he tries to decipher the odd sounds uttered by grownups and from there constructs some account of the shared practice of language. However, in the next paragraph, as Wittgenstein introduces his first language-game, the perspective changes considerably. In the example of the builders in §2, language is presented primarily as a tool for communication – as in the Augustine quote – but Wittgenstein shows how we can only understand the meaning of the words of the language-game of the builders if we understand the role these words play in their actions and the responses these actions give rise to. The builders' use of these words is thus a part of a mutual activity with the relationship between the builders at its very focus. Here, and in many other places in the *Philosophical Investigations*, Wittgenstein begins with relations between humans, describing their shared aims, activities, practices, and only from descriptions of this interdependency does he then proceed to describe the possibilities and actions of individuals.

The change from an individualistic to a relational approach to language is exemplified in many of Wittgenstein's remarks on psychological concepts, especially those surrounding the concept of pain. In general, Wittgenstein is criticising an influential tradition in philosophy that accepts various forms of Cartesian dualisms between body and mind and holds that the inner life of the mind is essentially *private*, in principle cut off from the other. Wittgenstein opposes this tradition by showing how the learning of the concept of pain is embedded in and dependent on a context consisting of our natural expressions of and reactions to pain, as we learn to make pain-assertions by developing the instinctive cry of pain into more complicated ways of using language. In doing so, however, Wittgenstein also brings out how the learning of pain-concepts is intimately connected to normative and potentially ethical ways of attending to the expressions of pain of others, taking them seriously or not, giving them comfort or not: 'A child has hurt himself and he cries; then adults talk to him and teach him exclamations and, later, sentences. They teach the child new pain-behaviour' (PI §244). Learning of pain-language is embedded in and intimately tied to the ways that grownups respond to the crying of children, sometimes in the form of help and compassion, maybe more rarely and definitely more dishearteningly with scorn or ridicule. Our understanding of the inner life of others grows out of the way we and others express this life and the ways we and others respond to these expressions. In this way, the 'human body is the best picture of the human soul' (PPF §25 [152]; cf. CV: 56 [49]; see Cockburn 2022 for an illuminating and detailed discussion of this remark).[7]

This remark is connected to a remark central to Wittgenstein's view of our relationship to the other: 'My attitude towards him is an attitude towards a soul. I am not of the *opinion* that he has a soul' (PPF §22 [152]). When we meet another person, we may form specific opinions about what that person thinks or feels, but we do not begin by making a judgement about whether or not the other in fact has an inner life, because, under normal circumstances, meeting the other simply does not raise any questions about this life. Our attitude towards the other puts in play the full concept of a human being, including for example their inner life, but the attitude is unmediated and does not depend on particular knowledge. Instead, this attitude is the *condition* of the possibility of forming specific opinions about the other – in this way, 'the attitude comes *before* the opinion' (LWPP II: 38). The attitude towards a soul is in a sense *given*, and it requires some effort on our part or some occasion on the part of the other to disregard it. As given, 'an attitude towards a soul' cannot itself be justified, but, as Peter Winch notes, it 'is in the context of a shared life ... that our *Einstellungen* towards each other can be understood in the way they are. That does not *justify* them, but it does provide the conditions under which they can be called *intelligible*' (1981: 14). Provided that Wittgenstein saw ethics as a fundamental part of human life, we may even speculate that these attitudes also involve an attitude towards the other as an ethical being, someone who

---

[7] When referring to part two of the *Philosophical Investigations*, I use the abbreviation PPF from the fourth edition (2009) but I also include page reference to the third edition (2001) in square brackets.

takes on moral responsibility and for whom moral concerns matters. If this is so, then such an ethical attitude conditions our relations to others, and any disregard for the moral standing of the other is thus secondary and requires some effort on our part or some occasion on the part of the other.

Wittgenstein repeatedly shows us how language grows out of and is dependent on fundamentally given and ubiquitous interpersonal relationships. That is, even if we seem to approach world, language, ethics as individual subjects, we are already embedded in and dependent on relationships to others that establish shared forms of normativity and shape our dealings with each other and the world. This holds for forms of instrumental and conditional normativity such as those involved in the praxis of the builders, but in the later writings, it also holds for what is best understood as forms of unconditional, ethical normativity such as those involved in our relations to children in pain. Throughout the *Investigations*, Wittgenstein thus investigates the ways that our concepts depend on our attitudes and relations to others, where others are understood not primarily as rational persons or abstract agents but as embodied, fragile, and interdependent beings. In line with this, Rupert Read has argued that Wittgenstein uses the so-called private language argument to show 'that others' pain and suffering itself addresses us *is* a relation between us, . . . a relation that is ordinarily direct/unmediated, though not entirely unfragile' (2019: 366). For Read, and I agree, Wittgenstein in the later writing 'situates us in our radical inter-involvedness. And that relates us *internally*. Such mutual internal-relatedness is basic – and yet vulnerable' (2021: 318; see also Christensen 2011b, 2015).

Wittgenstein also connects the relation to the other to the pursuit of self-understanding central to the later conception of ethics, for example in this reflection on his own ethical inadequacies: 'And when I now consider what others – who really were somebodies – had to suffer, then what I live though is <u>nothing</u> in comparison' (PPO: 183). Wittgenstein reminds himself that the demand to become better while bearing his lot in life is not unreasonable because others have met the same requirement in much more dire circumstances. The understanding of the suffering of the other thus establishes a non-negotiable ethical standard, just as it introduces a non-negotiable ethical demand. 'A cry of distress cannot be greater than that of *one* human being. Or again *no* distress can be greater than what a single person can suffer. Hence one human being can be in infinite distress & so need infinite help' (CV: 52 [45]). Wittgenstein presents the suffering of the other human being as the greatest and most terrible form of distress and thereby something that what must concern us ethically. A need for 'infinite help' is a need that we necessarily *have to* respond to – even a refusal to help counts as such a response – and as the need is 'infinite' it seems to raise an obligation that is at least in principle unlimited (cf. Løgstrup 1956 and Lévinas 1961; for comparisons with Wittgenstein, see Plant 2005; Christensen 2015).

Later in the same remark, Wittgenstein draws out how self-reflection may in fact threaten our relationships to others, noting that 'hate between human beings comes from our cutting ourselves off from each other. Because we don't want anyone else to see inside us, since it's not a pretty sight in there'. Wittgenstein continues: 'Of course you must continue to feel ashamed of what's within you but not ashamed of yourself before your fellow human beings' (CV: 52–3 [46]). Wittgenstein here seems to introduce a form of inevitable moral shame. When the suffering of other people places unlimited responsibilities on us, it becomes impossible for us to live up to these responsibilities and moral failure thus seems unavoidable. Still, Wittgenstein insists that we need to embrace and accept the shame that follows from this moral failure so that it does not make us hide or shy away from other people. Our main fault is not that we fail – because we obviously will – our main fault lies instead in our tendency to refuse to honestly admit and acknowledge this failure because this refusal isolates us and makes us turn away from other people.

The attempt to live ethically seems to require an (unsettled and unsettling) acceptance of our moral imperfections because only such acceptance will enable us to let the other person see us as we are. The relationship with others thus involves a twofold demand to accept, first, unlimited ethical responsibility towards the other and, second, that we will never be able fully to fulfil this responsibility. Such acceptance may seem almost impossible. Still, in the remark on infinite distress, Wittgenstein reflects, 'You can open yourself to others only out of a particular kind of love. Which acknowledges as it were that we are all wicked children' (CV: 52 [46]). The metaphor is striking by placing the idea of children, often representing innocence, together with the idea of wickedness, that is, the outright violation of ethical demands, and Wittgenstein's point seems to be that even though ethical failure is an irredeemable part of human life, we should approach this fact with the same readiness to forgive with which we would approach the missteps of children. Wittgenstein thus draws a parallel between love and ethics, implying that both types of relationships help us see our dependence and shortcomings, just as both require of us that we embrace these characteristics as inescapable features of ourselves as well as others. In other words, for Wittgenstein the demand to stay open towards others is a fundamental ethical demand.

The relational dimension of ethical reflection also stands out in a phrase that occurs several times in Wittgenstein's journals from a stay in Norway in 1937, first as a comment on his attempt to pray: 'After a difficult day for me I kneeled during dinner today & prayed & suddenly said, kneeling and looking up above:

"There is no one here." . . . But what it really means, I do not know yet' (PPO: 193). A few days later, Wittgenstein returns to the phrase. 'Now I often tell myself in doubtful times: "There is no one here." and look around. Would that this not become something base in me!' (PPO: 207). Wittgenstein repeats the phrase twice more, before its last appearance, about a month later: 'Today the sun rises at 12 noon & now appears completely. . . . There is no one here: But there is a glorious sun here & a bad person' (PPO: 231). Initially, Wittgenstein admits that he does not know what he means with this statement of absence, and the fact that it follows an attempt to pray seems to indicate that it expresses some sense of God's absence or even some form of abandonment. Wittgenstein does, however, distrust his own use of the sentence and hopes that repeating it will not 'become something base' in him, as if the simple expression of abandonment – or of independence – could be corrupting. Given his view of ethical reflection as relational, it may be that Wittgenstein sees this insistence on being alone, isolated from others, as itself an expression of ethical indifference. Still, it is crucial that Wittgenstein, in expressing his experience of absence, actually presupposes the presence of someone, the one he addresses in talking, the one told that there is no one there. Wittgenstein's saying of the sentence thus appears to be fundamentally contradictory; in one sense, he uses it to claim that there really is 'no one here'; in another, this very use reflects an insistence on the presence of someone, namely the listener, the one Wittgenstein is addressing.

This apparently contradictory attitude may help us to distinguish between two different conceptions of and relationships to the other. On the first conception, the other is a particular other – either a particular person or a particular conception of God – that represents specific ethical ideals or demands, while, on the second conception, the other is our *addressee* – the one with whom we are in dialogue about our ethical responsibilities and self-assessments. What plays an indispensable role in Wittgenstein's view of ethics is not the first, but the second conception of the other. Ethical reflection presupposes the relationship with the 'someone' that Wittgenstein is addressing, and in this sense, ethical self-understanding is essentially relational. For Wittgenstein to see and note that he (thinks he) is 'a bad person', he must have someone to whom he can address this judgement, even if it is only 'a glorious sun'.

In my view, the thoroughly relational character of Wittgenstein's later thinking carries great promise, even if interpreters have as of yet failed to get it fully into focus – maybe in part because of the tempting and influential picture of Wittgenstein as the lonely and singular godlike genius on the 5.15 train. It may be time to give up this picture. At the end of his life, what truly mattered for Wittgenstein seems to have been community and friendship – at least according to the moving anecdote by Norman Malcolm of Wittgenstein's dying words:

'Before losing consciousness he said ... "Tell them I've had a wonderful life!"
By "them" he undoubtedly meant his close friends' (1984: 81).

5.6 Coda

It is almost impossible to describe the significance of Wittgenstein's philosophy
on moral philosophy today. The exegetical question of how to understand the
Tractarian remarks on ethics is still ongoing, but in many ways, the later
philosophy has come to have a more profound influence in ethics. While
Wittgenstein was still living, it came to be a central source of inspiration for
what is now often called the wartime quartet, the philosophers Iris Murdoch and
Elizabeth Anscombe, Philippa Foot, and Mary Midgley. Through her friendship
with Wittgenstein, Anscombe introduced the quartet to his later thinking, and
their engagement with this way of doing philosophy in rather different ways
influenced the work they would each move on to do in moral philosophy (cf.
Cumhaill and Wiseman 2022). Wittgenstein's later philosophy also flowed into
moral philosophy through the work of Rush Rhees. He became a leading figure
in the 'Swansea School', a group of philosophers also including Peter Winch
and D. Z. Phillips that shared an example-based approach to moral philosophy
where especially literature was used to elucidate philosophical confusion
regarding the role of particularities in moral phenomenology (cf. Von der
Ruhr 2009).

The publication of Stanley Cavell's seminal work *Claim of Reason* (1979)
also contributed to the foundations of what we may today call 'Wittgensteinian
ethics' by unfolding the importance of a Wittgensteinian concept of 'the ordinary' in moral philosophy. In general, philosophers working in Wittgensteinian
ethics are critical of moral theories as well as attempts to generalise the diversity
found in morality or to justify actual moral reasoning in isolation from concrete
contexts. Instead, they take as their starting point the later Wittgenstein's focus
on ordinary language use and turn to contextual and particular features of moral
life, providing detailed description of the many ways in which moral considerations arise here. Some philosophers also draw on specific discussions in the
Investigations such as the rejection of the possibility of private language or the
remarks on rule-following (for an overview, see e.g. Christensen 2020a, 15–25).
Prominent proponents of Wittgensteinian ethics are Cora Diamond, Sabina
Lovibond, Raimond Gaita, and Lars Hertzberg, but today, the tradition is both
influential and widespread, covering philosophers working in most areas of
moral philosophy in most corners of the world.

References

Works Cited by Abbreviation

AWL   *Wittgenstein's Lectures. Cambridge 1932–3. From the Notes of Alice Ambrose and Margaret Macdonald.* Oxford: Basil Blackwell, 1979.

BEE   *Wittgensteins Nachlass: The Bergen Electronic Edition.* Charlottesville, SC: InteLex Corporation, 2003.

CL   *Ludwig Wittgenstein: Cambridge Letters.* Edited by Brian McGuinness and Georg Henrik von Wright. Oxford: Blackwell, 1995.

CV   *Culture and Value*, rev. ed. Edited by Georg Henrik von Wright. Oxford: Blackwell, 1998.

EN   *Letters from Ludwig Wittgenstein: With a Memoir.* By Paul Engelmann. Edited by Brian McGuinness. Oxford: Basil Blackwell, 1967.

LE   'A Lecture on Ethics'. In *Philosophical Occasions, 1912–1951.* Indianapolis, IN: Hackett, 1993, 36–44.

LC   *Lectures and Conversations on Aesthetics, Psychology and Religious Belief.* Edited by Cyril Barrett. Berkeley: University of California Press, 1967.

LWPP   *II Last Writings on the Philosophy of Psychology Volume 2: The Inner and the Outer.* Oxford: Basil Blackwell, 1992.

MWL   *Wittgenstein: Lectures, Cambridge 1930–1933. From the Notes of G. E. Moore.* Edited by David G. Stern, Brian Rogers, and Gabriel Citron. Cambridge: Cambridge University Press, 2016.

NB   *Notebooks 1914–1916*, 2nd ed. Edited by Georg Henrik von Wright and G. E. M. Anscombe. Translated by G. E. M. Anscombe. Oxford: Basil Blackwell, 1979.

PI/PPF   *Philosophische Untersuchungen/Philosophical Investigations*, rev. 4th ed. Translated by G. E. M. Anscombe, Peter M. S. Hacker, and Joachim Schulte. Oxford: Wiley-Blackwell, 2009/1953.

PPO   *Public and Private Occasions.* Edited by James C. Klagge and Alfred Nordmann. New York: Rowman & Littlefield Publishers, 2003.

TLP   *Tractatus Logico-Philosophicus*, rev. ed. Translated by Brian F. McGuinness and David F. Pears. London: Routledge, 2004 [1979].

WPC   'Wittgenstein's Philosophical Conversations with Rush Rhees (1939–50): From the Notes of Rush Rhees'. *Mind* 124(493), 2015, 1–71.

WVC   *Wittgenstein and the Vienna Circle. Conversations Recorded by Friedrich Waismann.* Edited by Brian McGuinness. Oxford: Basil Blackwell, 1979.

Other References

Anscombe, G. E. M. (1959). *An Introduction to Wittgenstein's Tractatus.* London: Hutchinson.

Boncompagni, Anna (2022). *Wittgenstein on Forms of Life (Elements in the Philosophy of Ludwig Wittgenstein).* Cambridge: Cambridge University Press.

Bouwsma, Oets K. (1986). *Wittgenstein: Conversations, 1949–1951.* Edited by J. L. Craft and Ronald E. Hustwit, Indianapolis, IN: Hackett Publishers.

Boyce, Kristin (2019). 'Logic, Ethics, Aesthetics: Wittgenstein and the Transcendental'. In Reshef Agam-Segal and Edmund Dain, eds., *Wittgenstein's Moral Thought.* London: Routledge, 133–52.

Cahill, Kevin (2004). 'Ethics and the *Tractatus*: A Resolute Failure'. *Philosophy* 79(307): 33–55.

Cavell, Stanley (1979). *The Claim of Reason.* Oxford: Oxford University Press.

Christensen, Anne-Marie Søndergaard (2011a). 'Wittgenstein and Ethics'. In Oskari Kuusela and Marie McGinn, eds., *The Oxford Handbook of Wittgenstein.* Oxford: Oxford University Press, 796–817.

Christensen, Anne-Marie Søndergaard (2011b). '"A Glorious Sun and a Bad Person": Wittgenstein: Ethical Reflection and the Other'. *Philosophia* 39(2): 207–23.

Christensen, Anne-Marie Søndergaard (2015). 'Relational Views of Ethical Obligation in Wittgenstein, Lévinas and Løgstrup'. *Ethical Perspectives* 22(1): 15–38.

Christensen, Anne-Marie Søndergaard (2018). '"Life and World Are One": World, Self and Ethics in the Work of Lévinas and Wittgenstein'. In Mihai Ometita, Timur Ucan, and Oskari Kuusela, eds., *Wittgenstein and Phenomenology.* London: Routledge, 248–72.

Christensen, Anne-Marie Søndergaard (2020a). *Moral Philosophy & Moral Life.* Oxford: Oxford University Press.

Christensen, Anne-Marie Søndergaard (2020b). 'The Philosopher and the Reader: Kierkegaard and Wittgenstein on Love and Philosophical Method'. *European Journal of Philosophy* 28(4): 876–91.

Cockburn, David (2022). *Wittgenstein, Human Beings and Conversation.* London: Anthem Press.

Collinson, Diane (1985). 'Ethics and Aesthetics Are One'. *British Journal of Aesthetics* 25(3): 266–72.

Conant, James (2005). 'What "Ethics" in the *Tractatus* Is Not'. In D. Z. Phillips and Mario von der Ruhr, eds., *Religion and Wittgenstein's Legacy*. Farnham: Ashgate Publishing, 39–95.

Conant, James and Silver Bronzo (2017). 'Resolute Readings of the *Tractatus*'. In Hans-Johann Glock and John Hyman, eds., *A Companion to Wittgenstein*. Chichester: Wiley Blackwell, 175–94.

Conant, James and Cora Diamond (2004). 'On Reading the *Tractatus* Resolutely: Reply to Meredith Williams and Peter Sullivan'. In Max Kölbel and Bernhard Weiss, eds., *Wittgenstein's Lasting Significance*. New York: Routledge, 42–99.

Cumhaill, Clare Mac and Rachael Wiseman (2022). *Metaphysical Animals*. London: Penguin.

De Mesel, Benjamin (2017). 'Wittgenstein and Objectivity in Ethics: A Reply to Brandhorst'. *Philosophical Investigations* 40(1): 40–63.

Diamond, Cora (1988). 'Throwing Away the Ladder: How to Read the *Tractatus*'. Reprinted in *The Realistic Spirit*. Cambridge, MA: MIT Press, 1991, 179–204.

Diamond, Cora (1991). *The Realistic Spirit*. Cambridge, MA: MIT Press.

Diamond, Cora (1996). 'Wittgenstein, Mathematics, and Ethics: Resisting the Attractions of Realism'. In Hans Sluga and David G. Stern, eds., *The Cambridge Companion to Wittgenstein*. Cambridge: Cambridge University Press, 149–73.

Diamond, Cora (2000). 'Ethics, Imagination and the Method of Wittgenstein's *Tractatus*'. In Alice Crary and Rupert Read, eds., *The New Wittgenstein*. London: Routledge, 149–73.

Diamond, Cora (2011). 'The *Tractatus* and the Limits of Sense'. In Oskari Kuusela and Marie McGinn, eds., *The Oxford Handbook of Wittgenstein*. Oxford: Oxford University Press, 240–75.

Engelmann, Mauro Luiz (2021). *Reading Wittgenstein's Tractatus* (Elements in the Philosophy of Ludwig Wittgenstein). Cambridge: Cambridge University Press.

Hacker, Peter (2000). 'Was He Trying to Whistle It?' In Alice Crary and Rupert Read, eds., *The New Wittgenstein*. London: Routledge, 353–88.

Hacker, Peter (2021). *Insight and Illusion: Themes in the Philosophy of Wittgenstein*, 3rd ed. London: Anthem Press.

Hänsel, Ludwig (2012). *Begegnungen mit Wittgenstein: Ludwig Hänsels Tagebücher 1918–1919 und 1921–1922*. Edited by Ilse Somavilla. Vienna: Haymon Verlag.

Hertzberg, Lars (2002). 'Moral Escapism and Applied Ethics'. *Philosophical Papers* 31(3): 251–70.

Janik, Allan and Stephen Toulmin (1973). *Wittgenstein's Vienna*. New York: Simon and Schuster.

Johnston, Paul (1989). *Wittgenstein and Moral Philosophy*. London: Routledge.

Kelly, John C. (1995). 'Wittgenstein, the Self, and Ethics'. *The Review of Metaphysics* 48(3): 567–90.

Klagge, James (2021). *Wittgenstein's Artillery*. Cambridge, MA: The MIT Press.

Kober, Michael (2008). 'On Epistemic and Moral Certainty: A Wittgensteinian Approach'. *International Journal of Philosophical Studies* 5(1): 365–81.

Kremer, Michael (2001). 'The Purpose of Tractarian Nonsense'. *Noûs* 35(1): 39–73.

Kremer, Michael (2007). 'The Cardinal Problem of Philosophy'. In Alice Crary, ed., *Wittgenstein and the Moral Life: Essays in Honor of Cora Diamond*. Cambridge, MA: The MIT Press, 143–76.

Kuusela, Oskari (2011). 'The Dialectic of Interpretation: Reading Wittgenstein's *Tractatus*'. In Rupert Read and Matthew A. Lavery, eds., *Beyond the Tractatus Wars: The New Wittgenstein Debate*. New York: Taylor & Francis Group, 121–48.

Kuusela, Oskari (2018). 'Wittgenstein, Ethics and Philosophical Clarification'. In Reshef Agam-Segal and Edmund Dain, eds., *Wittgenstein's Moral Thought*. London: Routledge, 37–65.

Lévinas, Emmanuel (1961). *Totality and Infinity: An Essay on Exteriority*. Pittsburgh, PA: Duquesne University Press.

Lovibond, Sabina (1998). Wittgensteinian Ethics. *Routledge Encyclopedia of Philosophy*, retrieved 7 January 2023, from www.rep.routledge.com/articles/thematic/wittgensteinian-ethics/v-1.

Løgstrup, Knud E. (1956 [2020]). *The Ethical Demand*. Oxford: Oxford University Press.

Malcolm, Norman (1984). *Wittgenstein: A Memoir*, 2nd ed. Oxford: Oxford University Press.

Malcolm, Norman (1993). *Wittgenstein: A Religious Point of View?* London: Routledge.

McGinn, Marie (1997). *Wittgenstein and the Philosophical Investigations*. London: Routledge.

McGinn, Marie (2006). *Elucidating the 'Tractatus': Wittgenstein's Early Philosophy of Logic and Language*. Oxford: Oxford University Press.

Monk, Ray (1991). *Ludwig Wittgenstein: The Duty of Genius*. London: Vintage.

Mulhall, Stephen (2012). 'Realism, Modernism and the Realistic Spirit: Diamond's Inheritance of Wittgenstein, Early and Late'. *Nordic Wittgenstein Review* 1: 7–35.

Murdoch, Iris (2003). *Metaphysics as a Guide to Morals*. London: Vintage.

Ong, Yi-Ping (2016). 'A Lecture on Ethics: Wittgenstein and Kafka'. In Michael LeMahieu and Karen Zumhagen-Yekplé, eds., *Wittgenstein and Modernism*. Chicago: University of Chicago Press, 206–29.

Phillips, D. Z. (1992). *Interventions in Ethics*. Albany: State University of New York Press.

Pianalto, Matthew (2011). 'Speaking for Oneself: Wittgenstein on Ethics'. *Inquiry* 54(3): 252–76.

Plant, Bob (2005). *Wittgenstein and Levinas: Ethical and Religious Thought*. London: Routledge.

Plato (1997). *Meno*. In John M. Cooper, ed., *Complete Works*. Indianapolis, IN: Hackett Publishing Company, 870–97.

Pleasants, Nigel (2008). 'Wittgenstein, Ethics and Basic Moral Certainty'. *Inquiry* 51(3): 241–67.

Ramsey, Frank P. (1923). 'Review of *Tractatus Logico-Philosophicus*: By Ludwig Wittgenstein and Bertrand Russell'. *Mind* 32(128): 465–78.

Read, Rupert (2019). '"Private Language" and the Second Person: Wittgenstein and Løgstrup "Versus" Levinas?' In Joel Backström, Hannes Nykänen, Niklas Toivakainen and Thomas Wallgren, eds., *Moral Foundations of Philosophy of Mind*. London: Palgrave Macmillan, 363–90.

Read, Rupert (2021). *Wittgenstein's Liberatory Philosophy: Thinking Through His Philosophical Investigations*. Oxon: Routledge.

Read, Rupert and Rob Deans (2003). '"Nothing Is Shown": A "Resolute" Reply to Mounce, Emiliani, Koethe and Vilhauer'. *Philosophical Investigations* 26(3): 239–68.

Rhees, Rush (1965). 'Some Developments in Wittgenstein's View of Ethics'. *Philosophical Review* 74(1): 17–26.

Rhees, Rush (2001). 'On Religion: Notes on Four Conversations with Wittgenstein'. *Faith and Philosophy* 18(4): 409–15.

Richter, Duncan (1996). 'Nothing to Be Said: Wittgenstein and Wittgensteinian Ethics'. *The Southern Journal of Philosophy* 34(2): 243–56.

Richter, Duncan (2019). 'Sketches of Blurred Landscapes: Wittgenstein and Ethics'. In Reshef Agam-Segal and Edmund Dain, eds., *Wittgenstein's Moral Thought*. London: Routledge, 153–73.

Schönbaumsfeld, Genia (2023). *Wittgenstein on Religious Belief*. (Elements in the Philosophy of Ludwig Wittgenstein). Cambridge: Cambridge University Press.

Stern, David G. (2004). *Wittgenstein's Philosophical Investigations: An Introduction*. Cambridge: Cambridge University Press.

Stern, David G. (2006). 'How Many Wittgensteins?'. In Alois Pichler and Simo Säätelä, eds., *Wittgenstein: The Philosopher and His Works*. Heusenstamm: onto verlag, 205–29.

Stern, David G. (2012). 'Wittgenstein on Ethical Concepts: A Reading of *Philosophical Investigations* §77 and Moore's Lecture Notes, May 1933'. In Hajo Greif et al., eds., *Ethics, Society, Politics*. Kirchberg Am Wechsel: De Gruyter, 55–67.

Stokhof, Martin (2002). *World and Life as One: Ethics and Ontology in Wittgenstein's Early Thought*. Stanford, CA: Stanford University Press.

Tejedor, Chon (2010). 'The Ethical Dimension of the *Tractatus*'. In Luigi Perissinotto and Vicente Sanfélix, eds., *Doubt, Ethics and Religion: Wittgenstein and the Counter-Enlightenment*. Berlin: De Gruyter, 85–103.

Von Der Ruhr, Mario (2009). 'Rhees, Wittgenstein, and the Swansea School'. In John Edelman, ed., *Sense and Reality: Essays Out of Swansea*. Heusenstamm: ontos verlag, 219–35.

von Wright, Georg Henrik (1969). 'The Wittgenstein Papers'. *The Philosophical Review* 78(4): 483–503.

White, Roger M. (2011). 'Throwing the Baby Out with the Ladder: On "Therapeutic" Readings of Wittgenstein's Tractatus'. In Rupert Read and Matthew A. Lavery, eds., *Beyond the Tractatus Wars: The New Wittgenstein Debate*. New York: Taylor & Francis, 22–65.

Wiggins, David (2004). 'Wittgenstein on Ethics and the Riddle of Life'. *Philosophy* 79(309): 363–91.

Winch, Peter (1981). '"Eine Einstellung zur Seele"'. *Proceedings of the Aristotelian Society*, New Series 81: 1–15.

Wisnewski, J. Jeremy (2007). *Wittgenstein and Ethical Inquiry*. London: Continuum.

Acknowledgements

I want to thank the numerous people with whom I have discussed Wittgenstein's philosophy throughout the years. I especially want to thank the editor for the Elements in the Philosophy of Ludwig Wittgenstein series, David Stern and two anonymous reviewers for helpful and insightful comments on a previous version of the manuscript. Earlier version of sections of this book has appeared in *Philosophia*, *The Oxford Handbook of Wittgenstein* (2011), edited by Oskari Kuusela and Marie McGinn and *Wittgenstein and Phenomenology* (2018), edited by Mihai Ometita, Timur Ucan, and Oskari Kuusela.

Cambridge Elements ≡

The Philosophy of Ludwig Wittgenstein

David G. Stern

University of Iowa

David G. Stern is a Professor of Philosophy and a Collegiate Fellow in the College of Liberal Arts and Sciences at the University of Iowa. His research interests include history of analytic philosophy, philosophy of language, philosophy of mind, and philosophy of science. He is the author of *Wittgenstein's Philosophical Investigations: An Introduction* (Cambridge University Press, 2004) and *Wittgenstein on Mind and Language* (Oxford University Press, 1995), as well as more than fifty journal articles and book chapters. He is the editor of *Wittgenstein in the 1930s: Between the 'Tractatus' and the 'Investigations'* (Cambridge University Press, 2018) and is also a co-editor of the *Cambridge Companion to Wittgenstein* (Cambridge University Press, 2nd edition, 2018), *Wittgenstein: Lectures, Cambridge 1930–1933, from the Notes of G. E. Moore* (Cambridge University Press, 2016), and *Wittgenstein Reads Weininger* (Cambridge University Press, 2004).

About the Series

This series provides concise and structured introductions to all the central topics in the philosophy of Ludwig Wittgenstein. The Elements are written by distinguished senior scholars and bright junior scholars with relevant expertise, producing balanced and comprehensive coverage of the full range of Wittgenstein's thought.

Cambridge Elements ≡

The Philosophy of Ludwig Wittgenstein

Printed in the United States
by Baker & Taylor Publisher Services